Applied UX RESEARCH

Bridging the gap between academia and industry for early career professionals

WRITTEN BY

UTKARSH SETH

ABOUT THE AUTHOR

Hi, I'm Utkarsh Seth and I wanted to take a moment to write the intention behind why I wrote this book.

My academic background is in Information Technology and Human Computer Interaction. During my Master's program at Iowa State University, I discovered the concept of "usability" and became intrigued by the field. I've always enjoyed listening to people and understanding their challenges, so I was delighted to find a field that allows me to do just that. My internship at Lenovo introduced me to UX Research, and my first job at Microsoft allowed me to fully immerse myself in the field. My current work at Google has really allowed me to look at UX Research from outside in and assess what works in the industry and what doesn't. This book covers my own personal views of the discipline and in no shape of form reflects my employer's views.

During my 17+ years in User Experience Research, I've worked on various consumer products at Microsoft, Google, and

Nordstrom, gaining a broad perspective on UX research. I've seen that while successful UX researchers develop essential skills over time, the industry's novelty can slow their progress. This book aims to accelerate that learning curve for new UX researchers by providing a comprehensive overview of the field, specifically how it transforms in the industry and what early career professionals can do to be better prepared for that transformation. It aims to bridge the gap between academia and industry to accelerate the onboarding time UX Researchers take, by giving them a view into what the practice looks like in the industry and what steps they can take to be better prepared.

I'm passionate about coaching and mentoring, and I want to equip new UX researchers with the knowledge I lacked when I started. This book is for those considering UX research as a career, pursuing education in the field, or seeking a more systematic approach to their current UX research role. The book also gives students and early career professionals a glimpse into the corporate UX research world. I share lessons from my own experience to help newcomers navigate the industry's challenges.

PREFACE

The world we live in today is increasingly shaped by digital experiences. From mobile apps that help us stay organized to websites that connect us with loved ones, the design of these experiences profoundly impacts how we interact with technology —and ultimately, with each other. At the heart of great design lies an essential practice: User Experience (UX) Research.

This book, UX Research - Bridging the gap between academia and industry, is your guide to understanding and mastering the foundational skills of this transformative field. Whether you're a budding designer, a curious developer, or someone transitioning into the UX space, this book is here to demystify UX research and empower you to create user centered solutions.

Why This Book?

I noticed a lack of books for UX Researchers, specifically those that bridge the gap between academia and industry. While resources exist for students and industry professionals, there was a noticeable absence of material to guide students transitioning into the professional realm. My primary motivation was to address this gap and create a resource that could accelerate the transition and lay out a clear path for students entering the industry.

In my 10+ years of teaching at Savannah College of Art and Design and mentoring multiple students and early career professionals in the industry, I noticed that most people wanted to prepare for the real world but did not know what that world looked like and therefore what steps to take to be better prepared. This book is an attempt to talk about UX Research fundamentals by sprinkling in industry knowledge throughout the book.

It is also my attempt to take all my knowledge of working in this field for the past 17 years and try to paint a picture of what it feels like being a researcher in a company. Along with explaining foundations of UX research in this book, I have also tried to incorporate real world examples to give the readers a taste of what the practice looks like in reality working in companies.

Who Is this Book For?

This book is written for anyone who wants to learn about UX research, including:

- Students and Career Changers: Those exploring opportunities in the growing field of UX.
- Early career professionals: Those who have entered the industry in the last few years and are trying to navigate the real world
- Product Managers and Entrepreneurs: Leaders aiming to align products with real-world user needs.

Whether you're starting from scratch or seeking to deepen your knowledge, this book offers practical advice, real-world examples, and actionable steps to guide your journey.

What You'll Learn

In this book, you'll discover:

- The core principles of UX research and its importance in creating user-centered designs.
- Step-by-step guidance on planning, conducting, and analyzing research.
- Practical methods such as usability testing, surveys, interviews, and more.
- Strategies for collaborating with teams, managing constraints, and delivering impactful results.
- Sprinkled throughout the book is how UX Research is practiced in industries and what steps can aspiring UX Research take to accelerate that transformation.

TABLE OF CONTENTS

CHAPTER 1:

INTRODUCTION TO UX RESEARCH

What is UX Research?

At its core, UX research (User Experience research) is the systematic study of users and their interactions with a product, service, or system. The primary goal is to understand user behaviors, needs, and motivations through various observational and analytical methods. UX research informs design decisions, ensuring that the resulting product is usable, accessible, and useful.

This explanation above is what is taught in schools and is true regarding what UX Research is from a core role knowledge perspective. All the academic knowledge that is taught, is about the core role knowledge UX Researchers have to build as a skill set to execute good research. The focus is on execution. However, one thing I had to learn from being in the industry was that along with knowing what UX research is from an execution perspective, it was also equally important to know what UX Researchers are accountable for which can sometimes be two different things and is a step change for people entering the profession.

Yes, UX Researchers are accountable for systematically studying users in as much perfection as possible and mastering the core role knowledge. However, when it comes to industries, UX researchers are also accountable for something more. See, UX Researchers in industries don't do research for the sake of doing research, or at least that isn't the primary goal. Research that sits on a shelf and does not inform product development is wasted research. Think about it from an organization perspective. Companies hire UX researchers to help them build and ship products and services and provide a user-centered lens that no other discipline (product managers, engineers, marketing etc) provides. Therefore, another, arguably more important thing UX Research is accountable for is to contribute to that cause and do research that ends up informing the products that the company is building.

This distinction and understanding of accountability is very critical as it lends a perspective when people enter the workforce. The perspective shift occurs when all of a sudden now the person not only has to implement what was taught in school and do good research, but also get adept in ensuring what they do ends up informing the product and making an impact.

This adds an additional layer of responsibility that extends the life cycle of research. While in academia research might stop with presenting the findings, in an industry, arguably that is where it starts. Once the research is done, UX Researchers then become accountable for making sure the research integrates into solutions that then eventually engineers build. Insights we collect from users don't sit in a presentation but actually change the designs and solutions to make it more usable and useful for the users. That connection between insights and how they change the product is paramount to creating impact. Therefore, producing insights becomes the baseline of what researchers are accountable for and then have to take the extra, arguably more important step, to integrate it into solutions. Note that in that follow up, there is no traditional execution of research, as taught in schools, that is involved - execution is already done. The follow up work requires additional skills like influencing, partners management, relationship building and prioritization. These are new skills people entering the industry now need to learn to build.

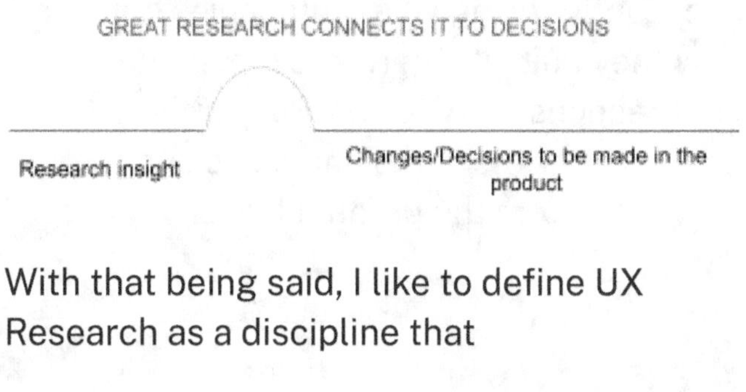

With that being said, I like to define UX Research as a discipline that

Informs product development through user insights, behaviors, needs, motivations and beliefs, by putting users at the center, to ship a crafted experience which is usable, useful and on brand

There are several important words in the definition above which are explained below

1. Informed - Many factors inform product development within a company. Business, marketing, engineering, and competition are all considerations that influence product and service offerings. Companies can choose to build products or services based on any or a combination of the reasons above. UX Research, which focuses on the user, is another important factor. It provides a unique, user-centric perspective that advocates for both current and potential users, influencing what companies build and how they build it. Therefore it becomes a core responsibility for UX Researchers to advocate for the users and make sure those insights inform the product like any other signal.

2. Ship - UX Research has a fundamental goal to use the insights it produces to inform the product that eventually gets shipped. UX research that does not in any shape or form make an impact on people, product or process is wasted and is little desired in organizations. Therefore, it becomes imperative for UX Researchers to ensure that the work they do actually impacts the outcome of shipping products.

3. Usable, Useful & on Brand - Usability, usefulness, and brand alignment are the three core metrics that can be used to evaluate the success of any user experience. UX research practices ensure that these metrics are measured and communicated to partners throughout the product development process in order to effectively convey the quality of the user experience that the team is building.

This definition aims to capture what UX researchers do and in an industry setting and what they are accountable for.

Problem definition vs Solution development

Another way to think about the role of UX Research is that researchers are responsible for problem identification that then informs the solutions designers create and eventually engineers build. UX Researchers master the craft of problem identification by understanding humans, what they do, why they do it and how they go about doing certain actions and behaviors.

The separation of problem identification and solution development is critical because those are 2 different steps in the UX world - the former done by UX Researchers and the latter done by UX Designers (or designers in general). This is the reason why while job hunting, there are 2 separate roles you might see online. However, in less UX mature companies, sometimes a single person which makes the role challenging does these roles.

Another reason why this distinction is important is because often both these paradigms are lumped into one and people are trained only to create solutions that can sometimes lead to not thinking about the problem first. Think about UX Researchers having the primary responsibility of identifying user problems, needs and behaviors and channeling them to designers and engineers to ensure that the solutions reflect the problems uncovered through research.

Why UX Research Matters - Don't build the ladder without finding the wall

Without UX research, designing a product is akin to navigating without a map. You can get from point A to point B but wouldn't know if point B is where you intended to be. The process becomes a guessing game, often leading to solutions that don't resonate with users. Without identifying the problem, the solution can still get built, but will not be useful to the users using it since it is devoid of the problem it is trying to solve. It is like building a ladder without first finding the wall.

Example: Developing a Fitness App without

Research: A company might assume users want a calorie tracker and complex workout plans. However, research could reveal users need a simple way to find nearby gyms or fitness classes, leading to an app that doesn't meet actual needs and has low user engagement.

This misalignment can result in:

- Poor user satisfaction with the product
- Increased churn rates where people will use it but probably not return to it since it didn't solve a problem
- Wasted development resources.

The Role of UX Researchers

As mentioned above, the role of UX research at its core is problem identification through a variety of UX Research methods. By identifying problems first, UX Researchers enable product development to be more objective and informed by user needs than being informed by people building it. Of course then those problem statements have to be communicated effectively to partners and translated into design decisions.

Because of this role, it is ideal that UX Research gets involved in product development right from the get go from initial idea generation. However, that isn't always the case in companies and I myself have had to build relationships to make sure I get involved early enough to be able to make an impact.

This is yet another shock people get when entering industries that all of a sudden they are brought into an environment where conducting research is not the only thing they do or are responsible for. Finding creative ways in making sure that research is the right research, collaborating with partners and driving results into the product to make an impact becomes a high priority item as well.

One thing you'll keep seeing highlighted and emphasized throughout this book is the importance of relationship building and collaboration with partners. Relationships are woven into the fabric of the work UX researchers do and is quite a step change when making the transition from academia to industry.

Key responsibilities of UX researchers include:

1. Identifying Research Goals: Collaborating with partners to define what the team needs to learn.

2. Choosing Methods: Selecting appropriate research techniques, such as interviews, usability testing, or analytics reviews.

3. Conducting Research: Engaging directly with users through studies, workshops, or surveys.

4. Analyzing Data: Transforming raw data into actionable insights by identifying patterns and trends.

5. Communicating Findings: Presenting results to teams and partners in clear, impactful ways.

6. Collaborate: Last but not least, collaborate with partners as frequently and effectively as possible to make sure UXR is always aligned with what the business is trying to accomplish.

If I were to stack rank these responsibilities, I'd say collaboration and relationship building with partners is by far the most important responsibility UX Researchers have. You will very soon find that relationships with partners is a fabric that is woven into almost every single aspect of what UX Researchers do and is crucial for a UX Researcher to be successful.

Just to list out some core UX Research responsibilities and how relationships and collaboration is woven into it are

1. Planning research and building a research plan - You'd want to make sure that the research plan is meeting the goals of the business and is going to produce impactful insights. This is done by active collaboration with the partners through meetings, sharing your research plan in a doc to get feedback and making sure that research is answering questions that will go on to inform product decisions.

2. Conducting research - While running sessions you'd want to make sure partners are attending the sessions and are hearing first hand from the users about their pain

points and needs. This needs collaboration and partnership.

3. Presenting research - While analyzing data and creating presentations, you'd want to ensure that you have shared the presentation for early feedback from the team before sharing it out more broadly.

4. Integrating research into design - It takes active partnership and collaboration with designers and product managers to make sure research insights are translated in a way that designers can use to make changes in the product.

As you can see, effective collaboration, relationship building and partnership with partners are all a core part of the role and are paramount in making research impactful every step of the way.

Skills of a Successful UX Researcher

There are several skills you can find on job listings which are crucial for UX Researchers to have so I have listed the ones which are often missed.

1. Empathy: Understanding user needs and perspectives. Building empathy takes genuine care and active listening and goes a long way when sitting with a participant to uncover quality insights.

2. Curiosity: Asking the right questions to uncover underlying issues.

3. Analytical Thinking: Turning data into actionable insights.

4. Collaboration: Effectively partnering with partners throughout the research process.

5. Communication: Presenting findings in a clear and concise way that helps bridge the gap between insights and solutions that need to be built

UX Research in Action

Imagine developing a new wearable fitness tracker. A UX researcher might:

1. Collaborate with partners to understand

the business goals, decisions the team is trying to make and appropriately scope out research that informs those decisions.

2. Share research plans with partners and ensure everyone on the team is aligned on what the research will uncover, what the non-goals are and what outcomes it will produce.

3. Conduct interviews to understand user fitness goals and what are people's problems with how they go about doing it now.

4. Use those insights collected to frame problems users are facing now.

5. Inform the design team of those problems to empower them to come up with solutions that solve the problem

6. Once solutions are built, test prototypes to observe how users interact with the interface and see if the prototypes are solving the problem identified in the first step

7. Analyze feedback to prioritize feature improvements with partners

Change in responsibilities over time

With all the responsibilities and roles described above, a way sometimes I like to outline the transition of a UX Researcher in their role from when they enter a company to when they become experienced is with the diagram below.

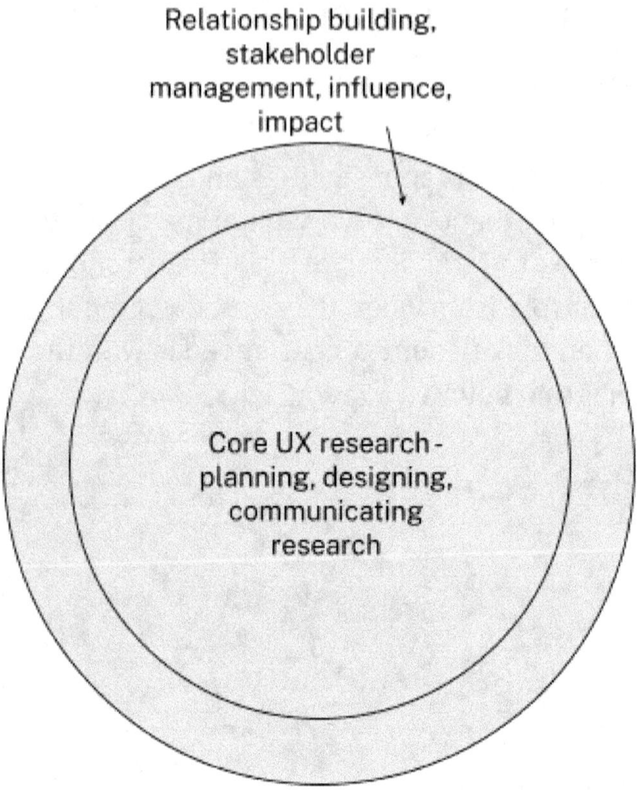

New in industry

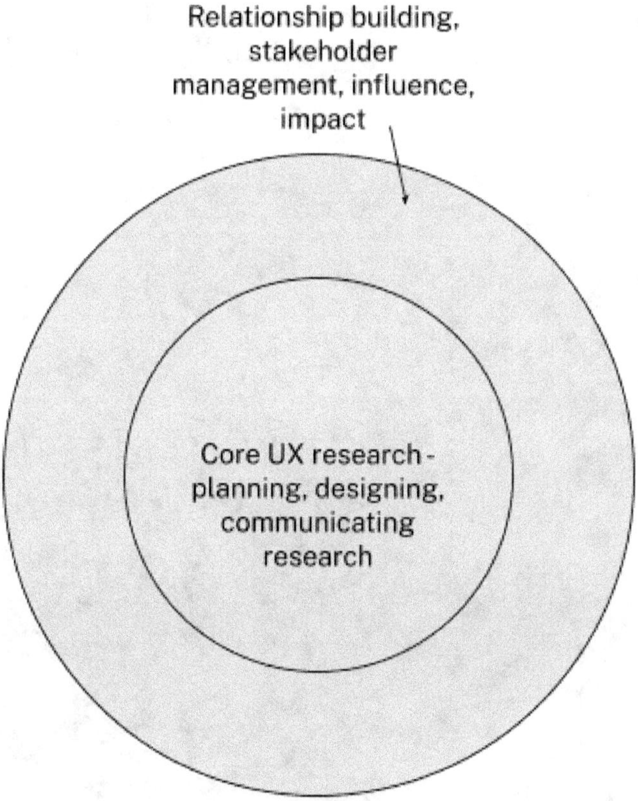

Mid level experience

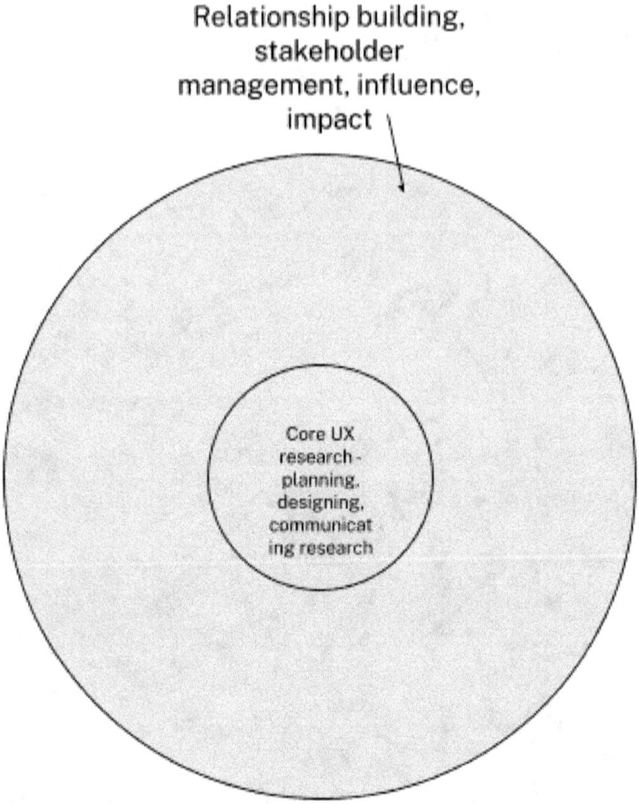

Senior or Staff level experience

Early in their industry journey, UX researchers often find themselves immersed in the tactical execution of research. They're busy designing studies, recruiting participants, collecting data, and analyzing findings. partners management might seem like a minor aspect, limited to presenting reports and answering occasional questions. This focus on "doing the research" is natural, as it allows newcomers to demonstrate their core skills and build credibility within the team.

However, as UX researchers gain experience, they begin to realize that research without influence is like a tree falling in the forest with no one to hear it. They discover that impactful research isn't just about generating insights, but about effectively communicating those insights to the right people at the right time. Gradually, partners management takes center stage. They learn to proactively engage partners, build relationships, tailor their communication style, and navigate organizational complexities to ensure their research drives meaningful change.

The shrinking circle in the middle doesn't

denote the time they spend on research but more around how they like to think about their role. The most successful UX researchers transform into strategic partners, shaping product strategy and influencing partners at every level of the organization. Through their work, UX researchers bridge the gap between user needs and design solutions, ensuring the product is both functional and delightful. Conducting research is still important but their mindset switches to influence and relationship building more than the execution of research.

The sooner people realize this and start making a shift towards this mindset the faster they can accelerate their transformation.

Conclusion

UX research is the foundation of user-centric design. By understanding what UX research is, why it matters, and the vital role of UX researchers, you've taken the first step toward creating experiences that truly resonate with users. As you move forward in this book, you'll explore the tools, methods, and strategies that bring UX research to life.

Let's dive deeper into the principles and practices that make UX research an indispensable part of design.

CHAPTER 2:

FOUNDATIONS OF USER EXPERIENCE

Understanding User Needs

At the heart of any successful product lies a deep understanding of its users. This understanding is the cornerstone of User Experience research. Users interact with products to fulfill specific goals, and their needs shape how they perceive value, usability, and satisfaction.

Identifying User Needs

Understanding user needs requires empathy and observation.

For example, when designing a meal-planning app, during the discovery interview phase, a user might tell you something along these lines

Meal planning is very hard for me because it takes a bunch of time just finding what meal I want to cook. I am a very good cook so that part is taken care of but finding what to cook is extremely hard and takes a bunch of time.

This tells us that the underlying need this user has is that they want an easy way to discover new recipes that they like.

Another quote you might hear is -

Once I discover what I want to make it is pretty hard to go back and copy paste a list of ingredients I need to go shop for. I have to copy paste everything I need into my grocery list which is time consuming.

This tells us that the underlying problem or the need this user has is to get help with generating a list of grocery items to shop for.

These needs can now be taken and framed into problem statements to make sure the meal planning app your team is coming up with has an easy way to discover meals that are relevant and a quick way to create a grocery list. Understanding these needs ensures the product resonates with its target audience, driving both usability and satisfaction. As you will see later, understanding fundamental needs and behaviors, while applicable throughout the research process, are more prominently sought during the early phases of product development.

The Basics of Human-Centered Design

Human-Centered Design (HCD) is an approach that prioritizes the needs, desires, and limitations of users throughout the design process. It's not just about creating functional products; it's about crafting experiences that users find usable, useful and on brand.

The HCD Process

Human-Centered Design typically follows these steps:

1. **Empathize:** Gain a deep understanding of user needs through research. This is typically the phase where the team does not know what to build and is trying to understand a

set of problem areas or user needs within the space. e.g. a company might want to invest in building fitness trackers but might not know what specific features to build or what designs to create. Empathize phase helps with this by discovering problems and needs users have with their current experience that then enables new solutions. This is where "generative research" comes in as you will see later in the book.

Example: In this phase a UX Researcher might go and talk to people who use fitness trackers to learn about their experience, what they like about it, don't like, why did they buy one, what motivated them to buy it etc.

2. **Define:** Identify core problems to address. Define phase synthesizes information collected from the previous step to now clearly and specifically articulate problems users have, needs they want to be met and behaviors they exhibit while using a product or service

Example: In this phase, UX Researchers will synthesize the information collected from the previous phase to now create problem statements for the team to ideate solutions on. A hypothetical problem statement could be "*Users were found to have problems with fitness trackers that took too many steps to start their fitness activity and wanted a quick way to do so*". Remember, at this stage no solutions or designs are built as the team is still trying to understand what to build based on user feedback.

3. **Ideate**: Brainstorm potential solutions. The problems from the previous phase are then taken and ideated upon to come up with solutions. It is critical that this phase of ideation is done with problems defined in the previous stage as the basis of solutions. Solutions, when defined without a problem, result in low usage and adoption as they don't fulfill a user need.

Example: Remember, the role of UX Researcher is problem identification which was done in the previous step. However, that doesn't mean that UX researchers disconnect at the ideate phase which is typically done by UX Designers. It is imperative that UX Researchers continue to engage in this process and ensure that the users and the problems that they came up with are well represented and the solutions are directly linked to those problems.

4. **Prototype**: Create simple product versions to test ideas. Solutions of various different fidelities (paper prototypes or fully functioning solutions) are created

Example: A UX Designer might come up with a low fidelity paper prototype of a fitness tracker or a completely functional one. The fidelity depends on what type of feedback the team is trying to gather at that stage of the product life cycle. Typically, the fidelity of the prototype goes up as the team gets more and more feedback from users and gets more confident in the solution direction.

5. **Test**: Evaluate prototypes with users to gather feedback. Those solutions are now brought back to the target audience to see if these solutions solve the problem that was identified in the empathize phase. This is where "evaluative research" comes in as you will see later in the book.

Example: UX Researchers will schedule a study with the target audience to see if the prototype the team came up with meets the needs and solves the problem identified above. Typically, step 4 and 5 are iterative that once testing is done, UX Designers iterate the prototype based on feedback for UX Researchers to study it again to see if the feedback is addressed.

Tip: Read about the double diamond UX approach

Key UX Principles

Several guiding principles underpin effective User Experience. These principles help UXers create products that users love while meeting business objectives.

1. Usability

A product should be easy to learn and use. Usability involves:

- Learnability: Can new users quickly figure out how to use the product?
- Efficiency: Can users achieve their

goals without unnecessary effort?
- Error Prevention: Does the design minimize the likelihood of mistakes?

2. **Accessibility**

Inclusive design ensures products are usable by people of all abilities. Key considerations include:

- Providing alternative text for images.
- Designing interfaces that can be navigated without a mouse.
- Ensuring color contrast meets accessibility standards.

3. **Consistency**

Consistent design helps users predict interactions. This applies to:

- Visual elements, like typography and color schemes.
- Interaction patterns, like button placement and navigation structure.

4. **Feedback**

Users need immediate feedback on their

actions, such as:

- Highlighting a button when clicked.
- Displaying confirmation messages for successful actions.

5. **Simplicity**

Clutter overwhelms users. Simplified designs focus on essentials, ensuring clarity and focus.

6. **Delight**

Beyond usability, great UX incorporates elements of delight, such as playful animations, personalized touches, or surprising easter eggs. These features leave users with a positive emotional connection to the product.

Conclusion

Understanding user needs, embracing human-centered design, and adhering to key UX principles form the foundation of exceptional user experiences. By placing users at the core of the design process, you ensure that your products are not only functional but also engaging and impactful.

In the next chapter, we'll explore the different types of UX research that can help you uncover user insights and drive your designs forward.

CHAPTER 3:

TYPES OF UX RESEARCH

To design user-centric products, it's essential to gather insights through UX research. However, your chosen approach depends on the questions you need to answer. This chapter explores the two major categories of UX research — qualitative vs. quantitative and generative vs. evaluative — and common methods within them that could be used to gather insights.

What is an insight?

Before we talk about types of UX Research, it is important to talk about a commonly used term in research - "Insights". It is often asked - "What is an insight?" An insight is a statement UX Researchers write by synthesizing data collected from studies that encapsulates user sentiment, user need, pain point or a behavior in a clear and concise way. An insight has several characteristics

1. It is new - An insight directs our attention to something previously unknown, or overlooked. This is why, to produce something new, it is crucial that the research done builds upon the past work in a space to avoid duplicating insights that are already known by the team. Doing extensive background research and using the existing knowledge to define your research plan so it produces new insights is crucial for an insight to be new. You'll know an insight is new if you can say "We used to think [x], but now we believe [y]". If research produces insights the team already knew, it devalues the work and the insights don't show impact on the product.

2. It answers the "Why" - Research studies produce insights into user behavior, which can be broken down into two key components: "What" and "Why." The "What" describes the actions users take with a product or service, while the "Why" explains the motivations behind those actions.

For example, in the context of a fitness

tracker, the "What" might be that 80% of users place their preferred fitness program on the home screen. The "Why" behind this action could be that users desire quick access to their favorite program to save time, especially when they've already begun their workout. Both the "What" and the "Why" are crucial for developing a comprehensive understanding of user behavior. One without the other provides an incomplete picture. For instance, knowing that users want quick access to their favorite fitness program is valuable, but without the "What," we wouldn't know the prevalence of this behavior. A complete research insight has both the components - What and the Why.

3. It is Clear - It is articulated in a way that the intended audience can easily understand and apply to decisions at hand. Crisp articulation makes an insight punchy and powerful.

4. It is People centric - It is written from the perspective of the user to demonstrate a pattern of behavior or motivations associated with behaviors.

5. It is Actionable - An insight informs a decision the product team is trying to make. This is often a problem in industries where UX Researchers produce good insights but fail to translate them in a way that can outline the next step designers need to take. A good insight directs the design and the product team what to do and what action to take as a result of it.

While writing insights after research is complete, make sure you have the above ingredients present. Producing insights that have these characteristics is paramount in making an impact on the product. Now that we know what an insight is, we can now look at different types of UX research and how those enable insight creation.

Qualitative vs. Quantitative Research

Qualitative Research

Qualitative research focuses on exploring user behaviors, motivations, and attitudes. It delves deep into the "why" behind user actions and often involves detailed studies. You can always ask "why" in a quantitative study. But because of the nature of how those studies are deployed, the answer to that "why" is often not as rich as what you get in a qualitative study. From an insight creation perspective, you'll need qualitative research to come up with a why.

Characteristics:

- Open-ended questions.
- Smaller sample sizes.
- Rich, descriptive data.

Examples of Qualitative Methods:

- User Interviews: In-depth discussions to uncover user thoughts and feelings.
- Usability Testing: Observing users as they interact with a product to identify pain points.
- Field Studies: Watching users in their natural environment for contextual insights.

Quantitative Research

Quantitative research is about numbers and measurable data. It answers the "what" questions, providing statistical evidence to support decisions.

Characteristics:

- Closed-ended questions.
- Larger sample sizes.
- Numerical and scalable data.

Examples of Quantitative Methods:

- Surveys: Collecting structured responses to identify trends.
- Analytics: Using tools like Google Analytics to track user behavior and usage patterns.
- A/B Testing: Comparing two versions of a design to determine which performs better.

Use Case: To optimize the same language-learning app, quantitative research might show which features users use most or where they drop off in the onboarding flow.

Reminder, this data as described is the "what" and you'll need qualitative research to identify why people drop off and what are the problems associated with the flow.

Combining Both Approaches

Often, qualitative and quantitative research complement each other. For example:

- Use qualitative insights to understand why users abandon a feature.
- Use quantitative data to measure how widespread the issue is.

Generative vs. Evaluative Research

Generative Research

Generative research is conducted early in the design process to explore opportunities and inspire solutions. It focuses on understanding users and their needs before creating designs. In the process described in the previous chapter, it is often used in the empathize phase of research. Since the purpose of this research is to generate problems, user needs, behaviors etc, it is called “generative” research.

Goals:

- Discover unmet user needs.
- Generate ideas for new features or products.
- Define the problem space.

Methods:

- Contextual Inquiry: Observing users in their real environment. Diary Studies: Asking users to record their experiences over time.
- Ethnographic Studies: Deeply immersing into user contexts for broader insights.

Evaluative Research

Evaluative research assesses the usability and effectiveness of a design solution once it is created. It typically occurs after concepts or prototypes are developed. Evaluative research comes into picture after generative research has informed solutions and they are ready to be evaluated with the target audience.

Goals:

- Test specific designs or features.
- Identify usability issues.
- Validate design decisions.

Methods:

- Usability Testing: Observing users interact with prototypes or live products.
- Surveys: Gathering user feedback on a completed design. Eye Tracking: Measuring where users focus their attention.

Both qualitative and quantitative research can be used in the generative and evaluative phase of the product.

Conclusion

Understanding the types of UX

research — qualitative vs. quantitative, generative vs. evaluative — equips you to choose the right methods for your design challenges.

Each approach provides unique insights, and combining them often delivers the most comprehensive understanding of your users. In the next chapter, we'll explore how to plan and execute a research study, including setting goals, recruiting participants, and creating effective research plans.

CHAPTER 4:

PLANNING YOUR UX RESEARCH

Effective UX research starts with meticulous planning. A well structured research plan helps ensure that your efforts are aligned with the project's objectives, involve the right people, and deliver actionable insights. This chapter walks you through the essentials of planning your research, including setting goals, identifying partners, and crafting a robust research plan.

Quick throwback to chapter 1 where I said that one of the things UX Researchers are accountable for is to show product impact from their research. It is a common misconception that executing the study with perfection has the most weight on the study showing impact - which is not incorrect. But the often overlooked part of research that has a higher weight on product impact is planning. The better you plan your research, involve partners, understand the decisions your research will inform, understand timelines by when the work needs to get delivered etc. the more the likelihood of it creating impact. All of that to say that be deliberate about planning your work as it is equally, if not more, important.

The UX Research process

While it is tempting to dive into the methods and learn about them, it is extremely critical to learn about the importance of research goals and questions as they dictate what methods and sampling criteria you should select. A research method is just a tool to answer the questions that need to be answered and changes based on the type of questions and your goals.

A research goal defines what you want to learn from the study and why it matters. The goals are then taken and expanded into more specific research questions. Who you talk to (sampling) and how you talk to them (method) is dictated by your research goals and research goals only and are steps that come after. A common pitfall when facing a redesign or a topic of research is to jump to methods which can lead to missing out on the question that really needed to be answered.

Think about it this way. Let's imagine you want to go from place A to place B. What modes of transport could you use? Jumping to a solution (method), say "car" might be correct but might not fulfill what you might be really after which could hypothetically be to save time in which case a "flight" as an option might be better.

On a more realistic side, let's imagine you were faced with 2 variations of an airline portal home page and asked by your team "Could you please through research find out which one is better?". Jumping to a method like a usability test, might be okay, but without knowing what the goal is might lead to unanswered questions. e.g. if the goal was to see which design has less problems in booking a flight, a usability study might be best but if the goal was to see which website's look and feel is better a larger sample survey would be the wiser choice to go for.

Goals and research questions do the same thing. They outline the intention of the study upfront which then dictates what methods (how) should be used to answer those questions. Never fall into the trap of jumping to methods directly without first outlining the research goal and questions.

This is also a trap interview question in many companies where an interviewer might pose a scenario and say “Which UX research method would you choose to answer [x]”. Many interviewees start their response by calling out a few methods without first articulating what the goals might be. When asked about this type of question, always clarify goals of the study and what are you trying to answer and then based on that decide what methods would be best to answer that question

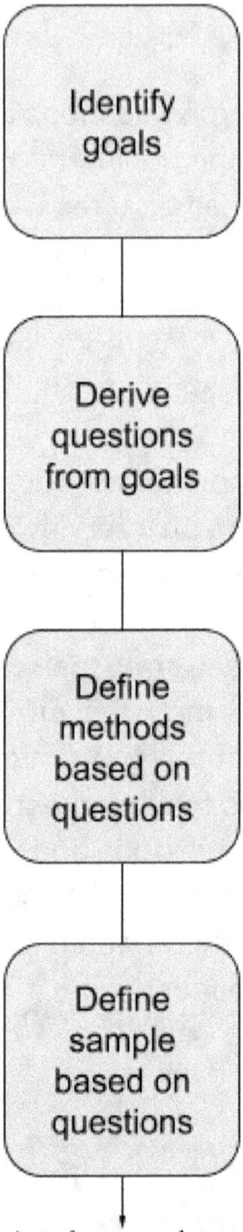

Remember to always choose methods and sample based on your research questions

Setting Goals and Objectives

The foundation of any successful research project is a clear understanding of what you need to learn and why it matters.

Why Set Goals?

Goals provide direction, focus, and a framework for evaluating the success of your research. Without them, you risk collecting data that is irrelevant or difficult to act upon. Another reason to set goals is because they define what methods and what sampling criteria you choose in the subsequent steps.

How to Define Research Goals

A key distinction when conducting research in an industry setting is that the research goals have to be tied with business goals to make sure that when research is done, the business goals are informed. This goes back to the accountability UX Researchers have to inform the product development process and one of the ways of doing that from the get go is to define goals.

While there is a lot that can be answered through studies, due to time and resource constraints, UX Researchers have to focus the study to target the key goals and decisions the product is trying to make.

Let's look at an example. An organization can come up with business goals for the year around the investments they want to make in their product. They could look something like this.

Business goal:

- Increase existing user engagement with our mobile app (measured by daily active users and session length) by 15% in the next 6 months.

If you are assigned as a researcher on this app and are tasked to do contribute to this business goal, here are some the topics or questions you might be interested in answering

- What is currently blocking user engagement with this app?
- What are the top reasons people leave the app?

- What features within the app enable user engagement?

In order to answer these questions you might come up with your research goals

UX Research Goals:

- **Understand current usage patterns:** Conduct analytics analysis to identify how users are currently interacting with the app, which features are most popular, and where users drop off.
- **Identify areas for improvement:** Conduct usability testing to identify any points of friction or confusion in the user flow. Are there any features that are difficult to find or use?
- **Test new features:** Conduct A/B testing on new features or design changes aimed at increasing engagement, such as personalized recommendations, gamification elements, or improved onboarding.

While another interesting question here could be "How do we attract new users to an app?", this is not a business priority or a goal for the company and therefore a question that'll be out of scope for your work. By integrating business goals you can focus your efforts to answer questions the business is working on.

Let's take another example

Business Goal: Reduce customer support costs by 10% this year.

Here the business is trying to reduce the time, money and resources it is spending on customer support. Here are some questions you might think about

1. What is contributing to customer support costs?
2. What does the end to end flow look like in a customer support journey and what are the friction points?

In order to answer these questions, you might come up with a research plan that looks something like this

UX Research Goals:

- **Identify common support issues:** Analyze support tickets and customer feedback to understand the most frequent problems users encounter.

- **Improve self-service resources:** Conduct usability testing on the website's help center, FAQs, and knowledge base to ensure users can easily find answers to their questions.
- **Test the effectiveness of in-app guidance:** Conduct A/B testing on different types of in-app tutorials, tooltips, and help messages to see if they can effectively guide users and reduce the need for contacting support.

As you can see from the examples above, your UX research plan directly now answers the key business questions your organization might have. This is also a great way to directly connect your work to business objectives and improve the overall business due to your work. partners collaboration and relationship building is a key way to understand business goals.

- Start with the Big Picture: Align research goals with business objectives and user needs.
    - Example: "Improve the onboarding experience for new

app users."

- Be Specific: Break down high-level goals into detailed questions. Example: "What steps in the onboarding process cause users to drop off?" As always, collaborate with your partners to make sure the set of goals you have outlined for your study are the right ones.

Before starting to plan your study, always make sure that you are talking to your partners to understand the business goal in order to focus your study to answer those goals.

Examples of Research Goals:

- Understand why users are abandoning the checkout process.
- Identify features that drive user satisfaction in a mobile app.
- Evaluate the usability of a new navigation system.

Identifying partners

As mentioned in the previous chapters,

collaboration & relationship building is the cornerstone of the role UX Researchers perform. This is where partners come in. partners are individuals or groups interested in research outcomes who are going to use the insights you produce to change or make decisions or change product design. Including them early ensures alignment, buy-in, and that the research addresses the right questions. Since research is never supposed to be done in a silo, think about your partners as the key group you need to work with throughout the research process in every phase. The more inclusive and collaborative your research is, the more the likelihood of it being impactful.

This aspect of a UX Researcher's role is also new to people transitioning into this space when they enter the industry. Academia teaches people on how to be great at conducting and executing work (which is very important) and industry brings a whole new lens to that role by infusing partners and relationships into the process of research. The more you can be mentally prepared for this change the better prepared you will be in your industry transition.

Key partners in UX Research:

- Product Managers: Define business goals and priorities.
- Designers: Use research insights to inform design decisions.
- Developers: Translate research findings into technical solutions.
- Marketing Teams: Leverage insights to align messaging with user needs.
- Executive Leaders: Support strategic decisions with research evidence.

The key to impactful UX research in industry is close collaboration with partners. Here's how to effectively engage them throughout the process:

1. Early and Continuous Alignment:

- **Initial Kick-Off:** Instead of just "involving partners," proactively schedule a kick-off meeting. Clearly define the problem, the business goals, and how research will address them. Discuss potential research approaches and get partners buy-in on the plan.

- **Understand Decision Points:** Ask your partners: "What decisions will this research inform?" "What information do you need to make those decisions?" This ensures your research is actionable and valuable.

- **Document and Share:** Create a shared document (e.g., a research brief) outlining the research plan, timelines, and key decisions. This keeps everyone aligned and provides a single source of truth.

2. Proactive Communication and Feedback:

- **Regular Check-Ins:** Schedule short, recurring check-ins (e.g., bi-weekly) to share progress, preliminary findings, and any roadblocks. This keeps partners informed and allows for course correction.

- **Visualize Findings:** Use visuals (charts, graphs, user journey maps) to communicate findings clearly and concisely. This makes the information more accessible and engaging for partners.

- **Invite Feedback Throughout:** Don't wait until the end to share findings. Actively solicit feedback at each stage of the research process. This helps you stay on track and address concerns early on.

3. Actionable Insights and Recommendations:

- **Focus on Impact:** Frame your findings in terms of their impact on the business goals. For example, instead of just reporting "users found the checkout process confusing," say "the confusing checkout process is likely contributing to cart abandonment and lost revenue."

- **Prioritize Recommendations:** Clearly articulate specific, actionable recommendations based on your research. Prioritize based on potential impact and feasibility.

- **Connect to Decision Points:** Explicitly link your recommendations to the decisions partners need to make. This makes it easier for them to act based on your findings.

Key Takeaway: In industry, UX research is about driving business impact. By engaging partners effectively, you ensure your research is relevant, actionable, and contributes to the overall success of the company.

Most of your time in industry is spent in talking to your partners, aligning on business goals, making sure the research you are doing is going to be impactful. Mastering the art of relationship building goes a long way in helping you advance in your career and making your work impactful.

Creating a Research Plan

A research plan serves as a roadmap for your project, detailing the methods, timeline, and resources needed to achieve your goals. It is typically a document created by the UX Researcher and shared with partners for feedback either in a meeting or through offline review at the beginning of a project. Progress is made on research only when all partners are aligned on the goals and are confident that the outcome of this work will inform decisions and impact the product.

Key Components of a Research Plan

- Research Objectives:
    - Clearly state what you aim to achieve.
    - Example: "Evaluate whether users can complete the checkout process."
    - Link the business objectives this research is going to inform through either copy pasting them here or linking to a company goals document. This serves as a reason behind why the research is being conducted and what business decision it will inform once complete.

- Research Questions:
    - List the specific questions your research will answer.
    - Example: "What steps in the checkout process cause confusion?"

- Methodology:
    - Define the research methods you'll use (e.g., surveys, usability testing). Remember to always identify methods based on the research questions.
- Decisions to be made
    - Collaborating with your partners, outline what specific decisions this research will inform. This is a way to make sure that the research is focused and the outcomes you will produce will have a high likelihood of creating impact. The more you know about the decisions at the end of the study, the better you can plan your study to focus on informing those decisions.
    - Example: If we know [x] from this study, we will change [y] in the product
- Participant Criteria:

- Identify the types of users you need to recruit.
- Example: "Users who have made at least one online purchase in the past month."
- Reminder - Your goals define the sampling criteria. If your goal is to remove problems for people who have already made a purchase use the example above. However, if your goal is to find problems with users who have never shopped on this portal before, make sure your sample also reflects people who are new to the site.

- Interview guide
    - Specific questions you would ask participants in your interview.
    - These questions are directly derived from your research questions above.

Logistics:

- Outline the practical details of your study:
- Timeline: When will research activities occur?
- Budget: What resources are required?
- Tools: Which platforms or software will you use?

Example Research Plan

Let's take a concrete example if you are working on a sign up flow for a mobile app.

- Objective: Identify pain points in the mobile app's sign-up process for first time users. This research will inform the business goal to increase app signups by 10% this year.

- Questions:
    - What steps are most confusing to new users?
    - Do people notice alternate payment options?
    - Where do people drop-off and why?

    - What do people like/dislike about the flow as compared to how they do it in other apps?

- Methodology: Usability testing with first-time users.

- Decisions to be made
    - If we knew that people are dropping off because of not finding the payment option, we will make those options more prominent on the page

- Participants: 8 users, aged 18–35, who have not used the app before.

- Timeline: 2 weeks to recruit participants, 1 week for testing, 1 week for analysis.

Tips for Effective Research Planning

Moving from academia to industry requires a shift in mindset. Here's how to effectively prioritize and plan your UX research in a fast-paced business environment:

1. Focus on Business Impact, Not Just Research Questions:

- **Academia:** You might have the freedom to explore broad research questions.
- **Industry:** Your research must directly address business needs. Use the examples above to tie your research questions to business needs.

2. Align with Decision-Making:

- **Academia:** Research often focuses on contributing to a body of knowledge.
- **Industry:** Research is a tool for making informed decisions.
    - **Example:** Work with product managers to understand their roadmap. If they're deciding between two checkout flows, design your research to compare those flows directly and provide data to support their decision. The better you understand the decisions to be made upfront, the better you can plan your research.

3. Collaboration is Key:

- **Academia:** Research may be more independent.
- **Industry:** UX research is a team sport.
  - **Example:** Proactively schedule meetings with designers, product managers, and engineers. Share your research plan, get their input, and ensure everyone understands how the research will inform product development.

4. Test and Iterate Quickly:

- **Academia:** Studies may have longer timelines and rigorous protocols.
- **Industry:** Due to resource constraints, research has to be done in a timely way to provide recommendations and next steps to the engineering team. Through partners communication, understand those timelines and make sure research is done within those timeframes.

Key Takeaway: In industry, UX research is about delivering actionable insights that drive business value. By prioritizing business goals, aligning with decision-making, collaborating effectively, and iterating quickly, you can ensure your research has a real impact.

While every step here is important, the one that I'd like to highlight the most is knowing the decisions upfront through close partners communication. I like to call it 'Start from the end". Understand, in as specificity as possible, what decisions your work will inform and refine/plan your research to make sure when you write the report the findings are indeed informing those decisions.

Here are a few questions you can ask your partners to make sure you have knowledge about those decisions upfront

1. What specific decision are we trying to make in the product with this research?
2. What will happen if we don't conduct this research?
3. What would we not be able to do if we didn't have any findings?
4. Let's imagine the answer to the question we're asking is [insert

hypothetical response]. What would we do in light of that?
5. When do we need the results to make sure we can still impact the product?

These questions are designed to anticipate future needs and obtain partners input to help you understand decisions early on. For instance, if you know your work will inform a decision about making payment methods more discoverable during checkout, you can plan questions that address that aspect of the flow to get participant feedback. Knowing the decisions in advance can help focus the study and ensure your work has a greater impact.

Conclusion

Careful planning is the foundation of impactful UX research. By setting clear goals, involving partners, and creating a detailed research plan, you ensure your efforts deliver actionable insights that drive meaningful improvements.

In the next chapter, we'll delve into executing your research, from recruiting participants to conducting sessions and managing ethical considerations.

CHAPTER 5:

METRICS & ROI OF UX RESEARCH

In academia, publications, citations, or conference presentations might measure the impact of your research. But in the industry, the focus shifts to **demonstrable impact on the business**. This is where UX metrics come in. They are the key to proving the value of your work and speaking the language that partners understand: the language of business outcomes.

Why Metrics Matter in Industry

Imagine this: you've just completed a comprehensive study on user behavior in a mobile banking app. You've uncovered fascinating insights about how users manage their finances and identified several pain points in the app's design.

Typically in academia the process of research stops here once findings are published. However, in an industry setting, research is not considered complete yet as it has not served its purpose - to impact the business. The questions still to be answered are

- How will these findings improve our app?
- Will these changes lead to more users?
- Will it increase customer satisfaction or revenue?

To answer these questions, you need **concrete data.** You need to show how your research goes beyond just findings and how it translates into tangible improvements in the product. This is where UX metrics become essential. They provide a way to measure the impact of your work and demonstrate the return on investment (ROI) of UX research. A statement you and your partners should be able to make to demonstrate that impact could be something like - “Because we now know [x] from research, which we did not know before, we have made [y] changes to the product, which has made the product [z% - metric] better.

This again goes back to the accountability UX Researchers have which is to show demonstrable impact on the product they work on. Research is not done for the findings to sit on a shelf but to concretely, with evidence, show how those findings improved the product and by how much. This requires systematic collection of data in your studies to show a clear before and after of the design and show how that data has gotten better as a direct result of your research.

Types of UX Metrics

UX metrics can be broadly categorized into:

1. Behavioral Metrics: These metrics track user actions and behaviors within a product or service.

Examples:

- **Task Success Rate:** The percentage of users who successfully complete a specific task (e.g., completing a purchase, finding a specific product).

- **Time on Task:** The amount of time users spend completing a task.
- **User Error Rate:** The number of errors users make while interacting with a product.
- **Conversion Rate:** The percentage of users who complete a desired action (e.g., signing up for an account, making a purchase).
- **Adoption Rate:** The percentage of users who start using a new feature.
- **Retention Rate:** The percentage of users who continue using a product or service over time.

2. Attitudinal Metrics: These metrics measure users' perceptions, opinions, and attitudes towards a product or service.

Examples:

- **Customer Satisfaction (CSAT):** Measured through surveys or feedback forms, CSAT assesses how satisfied users are with a product or service.
- **Net Promoter Score (NPS):** Measures

user loyalty and their likelihood to recommend a product or service to others.

- **System Usability Scale (SUS):** A standardized questionnaire that measures a system's perceived usability.

This chapter does not aim to delve deeply into UX metrics, their definitions, or collection methods. Many valuable books have been written on this subject. Instead, this chapter equips you with the most fundamental UX metrics to begin collecting in your early industry research projects. The goal is to familiarize you with these simplified metrics as a starting point, encouraging you to explore more complex metrics as your career progresses and the complexity of your space goes up.

A way to think about metrics is that they give us a way to speak to the success of a solution from a UX standpoint. It gives us a data informed way to say if the design met its intended purpose and if it improved what we set out to improve and by how much. Without metrics and hard data, the answer to the question becomes subjective. The team hypothetically would improve something but wouldn't know if it is improving the right thing and if so, by how much. Metrics give us a data informed vocabulary to say if the product is successful or not and if so, by how much.

Now let's talk about those fundamental UX metrics anyone can start incorporating in their usability studies. The reason we're talking about Usability studies as the method is because they are one of the most common study methods out there almost every UX Researcher conducts. I would re-emphasize that this is an oversimplification of the role metrics play in UX Research but worth noting as this is one of the easiest frameworks to get started with.

A product is successful when -

1. People know that the product exists. If people don't know that it does, there is no chance they will use it.
2. Once people know that it exists, & they want to use it, they can use it without any problems.
3. Once they use it without any problems, it proves to be useful for them and

they keep returning to it to fulfill their needs.

This is the most basic way to describe a product's success. Of course, there are other variables that go into it but from a simplistic standpoint, you can describe any product's success, or lack thereof, using these three sentences. If we go with this assumption, we can start mapping metrics to these statements that when measured will show whether a product is successful or not.

Statement	Metric
People **know** that the product exists. If people don't know that it does, there is no chance they will use it.	Awareness
Once people know that it exists, they **can use it** without	Ease of use

any problems, if they think it is appealing to them	
Once they use it without any problems, it proves to be **useful** for them and they keep returning to it to fulfill their needs.	Usefulness

A word about "Usefulness"

Useful, is a subjective word and therefore means different things to different people. What is very useful to one person might not be useful to another. A way I have used to describe usefulness is as follows

1. A product or a service is useful to people when it allows them to do/feel something they were not able to do/feel before

2. A product or a service is useful to people when they were able to do/feel the activity before, but this new service lets them do it in a [better, faster, more efficient etc] way.

Here is an analogy - Let's imagine a world where cars did not exist and people commuted on horsebacks. A company comes in and starts building cars and comes to its users and asks

- [Company] Hey, how do you go from home to work?
- [User] I go on a horseback
- [Company] How long does it take?
- [User] 40 minutes
- [Company] Hey, we have a product that can reduce that time from 40 minutes to 10 minutes. Would you buy it?
- [User] Absolutely

In the above hypothetical example, "usefulness" was created because this new product (a car) allowed the user to do something they could not do before -

commute from home to work in 10 minutes saving 30 minutes of time each way.

Now consider a world 10 years later where everyone had cars. Now let's say another car company went to its users and asked the same questions. Their point about getting the user from home to work in 10 minutes would not be appealing to the users anymore because they already have a solution that does that. Therefore this solution does not provide any new value. Users already have a car and they can go from home to work in 10 minutes.

However, let's say that this new company comes in and starts making cars in all different colors or starts making it in different sizes (SUV, convertible etc). Now even though this new product fulfills people's need of commuting to work in a similar time, it also gives them an additional subjective benefit that the previous solution did not - color, shape etc. All of a sudden this new solution becomes useful to users as it allows them to now feel/do something they weren't able to feel/do before.

Product usefulness is not very different from this simplified explanation. We use products that we perceive to be useful to us as they provide value that we either did not get before or if we did, this new one does it in a better way.

This is why measuring usefulness becomes very important in our work to assess not only whether people can use a product but also when they use it they find it useful.

How to measure

Now that we have our metrics, the next step is to operationalize them in your study and measure them. By operationalizing a metric, it means that turning the metric into a question we can ask in our research methods (surveys, usability studies etc) to collect data on it. The metrics below can be measured in a wide variety of research methods (with pros and cons) but for the purposes of this section, we will assume that these metrics are being measured in a usability study.

Awareness

Measuring product awareness in UX research is about understanding how familiar your target audience is with your product or service. It's a crucial first step in understanding user needs and behaviors, as it helps you gauge existing knowledge and perceptions. This can be done through quantitative and qualitative methods.

Quantitative methods often involve surveys and questionnaires with targeted questions. For instance, you might ask participants "Have you ever heard of [product name]?" or "How did you first learn about this product?". These questions can be scaled (e.g., "On a scale of 1 to 5, how familiar are you with...") to gather measurable data and track awareness levels over time. Qualitative methods, such as user interviews, can provide richer insights into *how* users perceive your product. Ask open-ended questions like "What comes to mind when you think of [product name]?" or "What do you think this product does?" or after having users try out your feature/product, ask them "before trying this out today, how familiar were you with this [feature/product]". What specific question you end up choosing depends on what you are trying to get out of measuring awareness. Think about the context of your study and the goal and choose the question that fits your needs the best. Another idea is to collect both qualitative and quantitative data and triangulate data to produce a more holistic insight.

Ease of Use

Ease of use measures how easy or difficult a product is to use. This metric is typically used at a task level when a UX Researcher is asking participants to complete a flow or a task within a product. After a user has completed a task, a way to operationalize this metric is to ask the question

How easy or difficult was it to complete this task?

- Very difficult
- Somewhat difficult
- Neither easy nor difficult
- Somewhat easy
- Very easy

As mentioned above, there are many more metrics that a team might be interested in like

1. Comprehension - Can people understand what is being presented to them

2. Discoverability - Can people discover the way how to go about doing a task

However, from an oversimplification standpoint, I have only provided Ease of Use as the metric. The reason behind this is that it is a generalized metric that tends to collect discoverability and comprehension type feedback from interviews. The way to do that is to ask people to explain their Ease of use rating and see if comprehension, discoverability, usability etc factors led them to rate it the way they did. In some cases, Comprehension and Discoverability become very important to a product and they separate that metric out to ask about it specifically as opposed to hoping people might bring it up within Ease of Use.

Usefulness

Measuring product usefulness in UX focuses on understanding the value users derive from a product or service. It goes beyond simply asking if users like the product and delves into whether it actually helps them achieve their goals and solve their problems.

This involves assessing the effectiveness, efficiency, and satisfaction users experience while interacting with the product.

On the qualitative side, user interviews provide rich insights into how users perceive the product's usefulness in their own words. Ask questions like "How has this product helped you?", "What problems does this product solve for you which you weren't able to do before?", or "What features do you find most valuable and why?". Analyze user feedback and reviews to understand what aspects of the product users find most helpful and identify areas for improvement. A question that could be asked in a usability study is

This [Product/Feature/Task] was useful to me

- Strongly disagree
- Somewhat disagree
- Neither agree nor disagree
- Somewhat agree
- Strongly agree

A very important follow up to this question is to ask "Why" and ask users to explain their rating to get richer feedback.

By having these questions in your study you can start getting a very basic idea about your product's success. As mentioned, these metrics are not exhaustive of all the metrics that are out there that could also be used but these ones provide the most simplified approach to measuring product success.

Now that you have these metrics, the question becomes

1. How to insert them in your study
2. When to insert them in your study
3. What method to use to ask these questions

As mentioned above, for the purposes of this chapter and to simplify the use of these metrics as you enter the industry, we will incorporate these questions into a usability study. We know that usability studies typically have small sample sizes, which is not ideal for collecting subjective data. However, we will assume that the goal of asking these questions in the study is to collect the "why" and gain a richer qualitative understanding of the reasoning behind people's responses.

Let's take an example of an interview guide

where the UX Researcher is interviewing users for a productivity app and trying to assess awareness, usefulness and ease of use.

Sample UX Research plan with metrics

Business goal: Increase user adoption of the productivity planner app by 10% this year

UX Research goal: To understand users' experiences with a new productivity planner app, focusing on awareness, ease of use, and perceived usefulness.

Target Audience: Working professionals aged 25-45 who use digital tools for task management and productivity.

Interview Duration: Approximately 30 minutes

Introduction (5 minutes)

- Thank the participants for their time.
- Briefly explain the purpose of the interview and how their feedback will be used to improve the app.

- Make sure their answers will be kept confidential.
- Obtain consent to record the interview (if applicable).

Warm-Up Questions (5 minutes)

- Tell me a little about yourself and your work.
- What are your typical daily work tasks and responsibilities?
- What tools or methods do you currently use to manage your tasks and stay organized?

Product Awareness (5 minutes)

- **Awareness Metric:**
    - I wanted to start with this question. On a scale of 1-5 how aware were you of this app before?
        - [At this time the UX Researcher records the answer. However, the researcher is more interested in understanding the why behind the rating and asks follow up questions]

    - Before today, had you ever heard of this productivity planner app?
    - If yes, where did you hear about it? (e.g., app store, social media, friend)
    - What were your initial thoughts or impressions of the app?
- What are your biggest challenges in managing your time and tasks effectively?

Ease of Use (10 minutes)

- **Ease of Use Metrics:**
    - Have you had a chance to use the app yet? If so, can you describe your experience navigating it?
    - Can you show me how you would use the app to [perform a specific task, e.g., schedule a meeting, create a to-do list]? (Observe their interactions and note any points of friction or confusion)
    - On a scale of 1 to 5 (1 being very difficult and 5 being very easy), how difficult/easy was it to

complete that task?
        - [UX Researcher records the score and asks follow up questions to understand the why behind the rating]
    - Could you please expand on why you gave it that rating?
    - [This can then be repeated for other tasks and participants can be asked to provide ease of use ratings for them]
    - Are there any features that were particularly easy or difficult to use?

Usefulness (5 minutes)

- **Usefulness Metrics:**
    - On a scale of 1 to 5 (1 being not at all useful and 5 being very useful), how useful do you find this app for managing your productivity?
        - [UX Researcher records the score and asks follow up questions to understand the why behind the rating]

- Could you please elaborate why you gave that rating?
- What are the app's most valuable features?
- Compared to other productivity tools you've used, how does this app stack up?
- Would you recommend this app to others? Why or why not?

As you can see, the three metrics above can be sprinkled in your interview guide to ask the participant about those, record responses and ask follow up questions. While 2 of those metrics are not suitable for a usability style study with low sample the intent behind that is to elicit a response from the users around the “why” behind it so it is still appropriate to incorporate.

Measuring demonstrable impact on the product

Note that all we have done so far is measured how easy to use the product is. We have not yet ensured that the design changes actually improved the ease of use of the product for that number to go up. The idea behind showing demonstrable impact is simple

1. A product is low on ease of use and has usability problems based on research findings
2. The design team takes those findings and fixes the problems identified
3. A follow up study is done asking people to complete the same tasks and are asked the same ease of use question
4. [If the design has improved] The rating for that ease of use question goes up because the design now has solved those problems that existed before.

To demonstrate research impact after the study is done, UX Researchers engage in the following activities

1. Run a study to collect awareness, ease of use and usefulness scores on tasks and the experience.
2. Setting up a research readout to present findings to the team
3. Translating those findings into decisions so design decisions could be

made

4. Setting up a follow up study to test the improved designs based on research
5. Replicating the previous interview guide and measuring those metrics again to record scores on the improved design
6. Hopefully, if the design has gotten better, those scores will go up.

A sample chart that could be created to show the trend could look something like this

Task	Awareness		Usability		Usefulness	
	Jun	Aug	Jun	Aug	Jun	Aug
Task 1	2.5/5	3.9/5	1.1/5	4/5	3.2/5	4/5
Task 2	2.3/5	4.9/5	2.2/5	4.2/5	2/5	4/5

This type of data visualization (or something similar) can go a long way in showing how UX Research, using standard metrics, can demonstrably improve the user experience of a product.

Bonus tip: It is highly recommended that the study is replicated again after the product launches to do a post launch evaluation to see how users are reacting to it in the wild and collect the same scores.

Since this research objective was tied to a business goal and it is seen that the UX metrics showed a positive uplift, there is now objective evidence that research was one of the factors that contributed to meeting that business goal. There could have been other factors at play as well (better marketing of the product, reducing sluggishness of the app by writing better backend code etc) but by doing these pre and post launch metric evaluation there is now demonstrable before and after UX metric ratings that show how the product improved from a UX standpoint.

Conclusion

Think of metrics as the bridge between your research insights and tangible outcomes. They allow you to:

- **Speak the language of business:** Communicate your findings in a way that resonates with partners and aligns with business goals.
- **Track progress and measure success:**

Monitor the impact of your design recommendations and demonstrate the return on investment of UX research.

- **Iterate and improve:** Use data to identify areas for improvement and make data-informed decisions about product development.

Embracing metrics requires a shift in mindset, a move from purely theoretical exploration to applied research that drives real-world impact. It's about understanding that UX research in industry is not just about uncovering insights, but also about demonstrating the value of those insights and contributing to the bottom line.

As you embark on your UX journey, remember that metrics are your allies. They are the tools that empower you to make a real difference in users' lives and contribute to the success of the products and services you help create. So, embrace the power of metrics, and let your research make a lasting impact on the products you work on.

CHAPTER 6:

RESEARCH METHODS

Effective UX research relies on a variety of methods to gather insights about users and their experiences. Each method has its strengths and is suited to different stages of the research process.

This chapter explores some widely used research methods within the industry. There are many books out there that talk about methods in general but I wanted to highlight a few I have seen UX Researchers use relatively more often in a company.

Usability Testing

Usability testing is an evaluative research method that evaluates how easily users can complete tasks with a product. The goal of a usability test is to identify problems and pain points in a certain UI or flow. Because the focus is to find problems, a typical sample size for this study is between 5-8 users. You can add more users in your study but the ROI of finding new problems plateaus after 9-10 users.

Tip: Search online for “minimum sample size for usability studies”

How It Works:

- Define research goals, questions and target audience for your study.
- Recruit participants who match your target audience.
- Design an interview guide with tasks you would like users to complete in your product
- Assign them specific tasks to perform (e.g., “Search for and purchase a product”).
- Observe their interactions, note where they struggle and ask follow up open ended questions
- Collect metrics and report insights

User Interviews

User interviews involve one-on-one conversations with users to understand their behaviors, motivations, and pain points. User interviews is a bit of a confusing term to use as technically speaking a usability study can also be a user interview. However, this term is broadly used in the industry to talk about a method where there is no UI involved and the conversation with the user largely remains open-ended to uncover their behaviors, needs etc on a certain topic. Therefore, user interviews fall in the "generative" research methodology.

How It Works:

- Prepare open-ended questions focused on your research goals.
- Engage in a structured yet conversational dialogue. Analyze recurring themes and patterns.

Example:

A fitness app developer conducts interviews to understand why users cancel subscriptions. Note that this question does not necessarily have any UI involved and the interviewer just generally wants to know what motivates people to cancel subscriptions. The interview can definitely steer towards asking users to show UI where they have done so but the goal of the conversation is to uncover behaviors, motivations and needs without showing them any solutions. Key questions include:

Surveys and Questionnaires

These tools gather large-scale feedback by asking users structured questions, often using multiple-choice or rating scales. Surveys fall into the Quantitative research methodology. This also goes back to the "What" and the "Why" of an insight. Surveys, being a quantitative method, uncover the "What". One way to think about the difference between usability tests and surveys is this. Imagine you are working on an airline website and your goal is to find out problems people have while booking a flight. Since the goal is problem identification with a UI, a usability study is perfect for that setting since that method specializes in finding problems with a UI. On the other hand, let's imagine the goal of the study is to find out whether users like a blue background or a pink background on the website. This changes the goal of the study from finding problems to identifying subjective preferences. We can't talk to a small sample of 8 users and decide which color people like more. The decision here is subjective to personal taste and just talking to 8 people won't get us the answer.

Any time researchers are trying to get an answer to a preference, a larger sample is taken into account for the target audience to get a definitive answer. Another example where a survey might be helpful is for the question - Which tools people use the most to find out about new TV shows and movies. A usability test here might not be beneficial since 8 people won't give us an answer that could be generalized to a larger population and we'll have to do a survey instead to answer the question.

How It Works:

- Similar to any research method, define a clear research goal and make sure survey is the right method to answer that goal. (e.g., "Assess user satisfaction with our mobile app").
- Distribute the survey via email, social media, or in-app prompts.
- Analyze quantitative and qualitative responses.

While surveys are somewhat common in an academic setting, they become one of the more prominent methods in an industry setting. Learning and applying basic statistical skills in your classwork or in your early career days will go a long way in getting you up to speed with this method.

Maxdiff

UX Researchers often find themselves in discussions (more often during product definition phase when teams are thinking about what to build) where they have a list of items that the team needs prioritization around. The intent behind the prioritization could be many

1. Team does not have enough resources to build all the features and want to use user input in deciding which items to build
2. Team does not know which features are going to be most useful to build and want user input
3. UX Researchers have identified 10-20 user journeys or pain points in a product and want to prioritize or stack rank them based on a metric

Think about being in a situation where you have multiple product features or multiple items (user journeys, user problems etc) and you need to provide a view around which one is the most important (or problematic, or frequent, or any other metric). As mentioned above, there is a lot of work to do in organizations and not enough resources to do it and teams are constantly prioritizing things across the board. This is where a method called “Maxdiff” comes in that is used pretty extensively in companies by UX Researchers to understand user preferences.

This technique, also known as "best-worst scaling," helps us uncover the relative importance users place on different attributes, features, or design elements.

Why MaxDiff?

Imagine you're designing a new mobile banking app. You brainstorm a plethora of potential features: budgeting tools, peer-to-peer payments, investment options, personalized financial advice, and more. How do you determine which features truly resonate with your target audience and should be prioritized for development? Traditional rating scales can fall short, as users tend to rate many features as "important." MaxDiff comes to the rescue by forcing users to make trade-offs, revealing their true priorities.

How MaxDiff Works

The core of MaxDiff lies in presenting respondents with small sets of items (usually 3-5) from a larger list and asking them to identify the "best" and "worst" within each set. By repeating this process with different combinations of items, we gather valuable data on relative preferences.

Example:

Let's revisit our mobile banking app. We might present a user with this set:

- Budgeting tools
- Investment options
- Bill pay reminders
- ATM locator

The user might choose "Investment options" as the most important and "ATM locator" as the least important. By analyzing responses across many users and item combinations, we can generate a score for each feature, reflecting its relative importance to the target audience.

Analyzing MaxDiff Data

Specialized software, like Sawtooth Software or R packages, helps analyze MaxDiff data. The output typically includes:

- **Individual level scores:** Preference scores for each item for each respondent.
- **Segment level scores:** Identifying groups of users with similar preference patterns.

- **Attribute importance:** Overall ranking of items based on their relative preference scores.

You can use the same method to prioritize other things as well like user problems, user journeys etc.

Advantages of MaxDiff

- **Reduces response bias:** Forces users to make trade-offs, minimizing the tendency to rate everything as important.
- **Provides granular insights:** Reveals fine-grained distinctions in preferences, even among seemingly similar items.
- **Versatile applications:** Applicable to a wide range of research questions, from product development to user interface design to marketing.

Key Takeaways

MaxDiff is a valuable tool for uncovering user preferences and prioritizing features or attributes. By understanding this technique, you'll be well-equipped to tackle complex research challenges and contribute to creating user-centered products and experiences.

So, there you have it – a primer on MaxDiff! As you venture further into the world of UX research, remember the power of this method to unlock the secrets of user preferences and drive impactful design decisions.

Contextual Inquiry

Contextual inquiry, a generative and qualitative method, involves observing users in their natural environment to understand their workflows, behaviors, and pain points. Contextual inquiry is also a "user interview" and it also focuses on understanding people's behaviors and needs. The difference here and why it is called "contextual" is because this interview happens in the context of where people are - their home, work or where the experience is supposed to be used.

How It Works:

- Visit users in their environment (e.g., homes, workplaces). Watch them interact with the product or perform related tasks.
- Ask clarifying questions to understand their thought process.

Example:

- A retailer might want to understand how users shop in a store. UX Researchers do a shop along study with potential customers and observe them while they navigate the store.

Findings:

- Many users had questions about item sizes and availability and struggled to find customer service people inside the store leading to abandoning their shopping journey.

Diary study

Another widely used tool in business is diary study. This method allows you to observe user behavior over a period of time as opposed to a usability study or an interview where you speak to users in a snapshot of time

Choosing the Right Method

Please refer to the UX Research process chapter above to get a refresher on how to choose the right method. A quick reminder - the goals and research questions of your research define what method you choose. While there is some flexibility within the methods, we can't really pick a method of our liking and it has to be tied to what we're trying to accomplish from the work. Every time you choose a method, make sure it is tied to what the research question is and if the method is suited to answer that research question. Jumping to selecting a method, without first identifying the research question will lead to incorrect or incomplete answers.

Each research method has unique strengths and is used based on the type of research question you are trying to answer.

- Use Usability Testing to identify

barriers in task completion. Conduct User Interviews to explore motivations and feelings.

- Deploy Surveys to gather large-scale feedback.
- Use Card Sorting to structure content effectively.
- Run A/B Tests to validate design decisions.
- Perform Contextual Inquiries for authentic insights into real world use.

Combining methods often provides the most comprehensive understanding of user needs and behaviors.

Conclusion

Understanding and applying various research methods ensures your UX efforts are grounded in user insights. By tailoring the method to the research question, you can gather actionable data that drives meaningful design improvements.

In the next chapter, we'll explore how to recruit participants, build user personas, and manage logistics for effective research.

CHAPTER 7:

RECRUITING PARTICIPANTS

Recruiting the right participants is crucial to the success of UX research. Whether you're conducting usability tests, interviews, or surveys, the quality of your insights depends on the relevance of your participants. In this chapter, we'll explore how to find the right users, build user personas, and manage participant logistics effectively.

Finding the Right Users

Why Participant Selection Matters

Selecting the right participants ensures your research reflects the real-world behaviors, needs, and challenges of your target audience. Testing with the wrong users can lead to irrelevant or misleading insights.

Remember, your study and data you produce is only as good as the participants you talk to. For example - if you're trying to see how new users who have never used your service react to your product but you end up recruiting existing ones or ones who have no interest in it, your data will uncover findings that will be incorrect or of no use to you.

Steps to Find the Right Users

Define Your Target Audience:

- Use your product's user base or intended audience as a starting point. Your research goals and questions will define who you end up talking to. Clearly write your goals to include users who you intend to talk to and ones that are in your non-goals.

- Example: For an app targeting freelancers, focus on participants who work independently and use digital tools daily. However, if the goal of the study is to see why people are not doing more freelancing, talk to people who have high interest in becoming freelancers but haven't made the move yet. Who you talk to depends on what your research goal is.

Screen Participants:

- Use a screener survey to filter participants based on criteria such as:
    - Demographics (age, location, gender).
    - Behaviors (frequency of product use, familiarity with similar tools).
    - Goals and challenges.
    - Example Question: "How often do you use online project management tools?" (Never, Occasionally, Daily).

Leverage Recruitment Channels:

- Existing Customers: Reach active users via email or in-app notifications.
- Social Media: Post calls for participants on platforms like LinkedIn, Twitter, or Facebook.
- Recruitment Agencies: Use professional services to find

participants who match your criteria.
- Online Panels: Platforms like UserTesting or Respondent.io can quickly connect you with potential participants.

Offer Incentives:

Incentives encourage participation and show appreciation for users' time. Options include:
- Gift cards.
- Discounts on your product.
- Monetary compensation.

Building User Personas

User personas are fictional representations of your target users based on research data. They help guide design decisions by focusing on real user needs.

Creating Effective Personas

- Gather Data: Use insights from user research, surveys, and analytics to understand your audience.
- Define Key Attributes:

- Demographics: Age, occupation, education level, location.
- Behaviors: How they interact with similar products or services.
- Goals: What they want to achieve with your product. Pain Points: Challenges or frustrations they face.
- Develop Persona Profiles: Create detailed profiles describing the users and their motivations.

Example Persona:

- Name: Sarah Johnson
- Age: 34
- Occupation: Freelance Graphic Designer
- Goals:
- Stay organized while managing multiple client projects. Easily track income and expenses.
- Pain Points:
- Finds most project management tools too complex. Struggles to track deadlines across different platforms. Behaviors:
- Uses digital tools daily, prefers mobile-friendly apps.

Benefits of Personas:

- Align teams around a shared understanding of users.
- Prioritize features that address key pain points.
- Avoid designing for hypothetical "general users."
- Personas also give your product team a human way to design solutions.

Not all projects require persona building and it depends on how large your area is or how unknown your users are among your product team. This effort can take some time if done diligently so prioritize personas with your product team and understand how/when it fits in your timeline.

Managing Participant Logistics

Scheduling Sessions

Efficient scheduling is essential to ensure your research runs smoothly.

- Use Scheduling Tools: Platforms like Calendly or Doodle simplify booking

sessions.
- Offer Flexible Options: Provide multiple time slots to accommodate participants' availability.
- Send Reminders: Use email or text reminders to reduce no shows.

Providing Clear Instructions

Ensure participants know what to expect by sharing:

- Session Details: Date, time, duration, and location (or virtual meeting link).
- Requirements: Devices or software needed (e.g., a laptop with a webcam).
- Session Goals: A brief explanation of what they'll be doing.

Handling Compensation

- Communicate Early: Let participants know what they'll receive and when.
- Keep It Simple: Use platforms like PayPal or gift card services for seamless delivery.
- Follow Up Promptly: Distribute compensation within the promised

timeline to maintain trust.

Backup Plans

Unforeseen issues can arise, so always have a contingency plan: Recruit extra participants to account for dropouts. Prepare alternative activities if technical issues occur. Schedule buffer time between sessions for flexibility.

Example Scenario: Recruiting for a Usability Test

A team developing a meal-planning app wants to test their new recipe search feature.

- Define Target Users based on your research goals and questions
    - Home cooks aged 25–45.
    - Regularly cook at least 3 meals per week.
    - Use mobile apps for recipes.
- Create Screener Survey:
    - “How often do you use recipe apps?” (Never, Rarely, Sometimes, Often).
    - “What is your primary device for cooking-related tasks?” (Phone,

Tablet, Computer).

- Recruit Participants:
    - Post a call for participants on cooking forums and social media.
    - Use a recruitment service to find qualified users.
- Manage Logistics:
    - Schedule 10 participants for 30-minute virtual usability sessions over Zoom.
    - Send instructions and reminders with session links. Compensate participants with $25 gift cards after the session.

Conclusion

Recruiting participants is a critical step in UX research. By finding the right users, building personas to understand their needs, and managing logistics efficiently, you ensure your research delivers meaningful and actionable insights.

In the next chapter, we'll dive into conducting research sessions, including preparing for sessions, moderating effectively, and addressing ethical considerations.

CHAPTER 8:

CONDUCTING RESEARCH

Once you've planned your study and recruited participants, it's time to conduct your research. This phase requires careful preparation, skilled moderation, and adherence to ethical guidelines to ensure the process runs smoothly and delivers valuable insights. This chapter will guide you through preparing for sessions, employing effective moderation techniques, and addressing ethical considerations in UX research.

Preparing for Sessions

1. Define Objectives Clearly

Before starting, revisit the research goals. Ensure you and your team are aligned on:

- What you hope to learn.

- How the insights will inform design decisions. This is a key departure in how you run studies in the industry.

  Here are the scenarios you are trying to avoid

  - Research readout is done and now the team is wondering how to apply the findings to inform decisions
  - Research is done and it reiterated the findings team already knew about from past work
  - Research is done and it touched upon the decisions but did not completely answer them

These scenarios make research efforts go down the drain as the work fails to produce impact. Remember the accountability UX Researchers have - to create impact on the product. Almost all of these scenarios could be avoided if there is upfront work that is done during planning to specifically understand the decisions the team is trying to make.

Example: If you're testing a new checkout

process, the objective might be to identify barriers preventing users from completing their purchases.

2. Choose the Right Tools

Select tools and platforms based on the type of research:

- Remote Sessions: Tools like Zoom, Lookback, or Microsoft Teams.
- In-Person Sessions: Physical spaces with necessary equipment (e.g., recording devices).
- Surveys/Questionnaires: Platforms like Google Forms, Typeform, or Qualtrics.

3. Prepare Materials

Ensure all materials are ready and tested beforehand, including:

- Prototypes or products for participants to interact with. A script or guide outlining the session structure.
- Notebooks, digital recording tools, or observation sheets.

Tip: Test prototypes to ensure functionality and reliability during the session.

4. Conduct a Pilot Test

Run a trial session with colleagues or a small group of users to:

- Identify potential issues with tasks or materials.
- Refine the session flow and timing.

I cannot emphasize the importance of pilot studies enough. They are extremely valuable in finding blind spots in your flow or prototype which you may not have anticipated before. The feedback you get from these sessions goes directly in making your plan better thereby making sure the sessions you do go smoothly.

5. Create a Comfortable Environment

- For in-person sessions: Set up a quiet, distraction-free space with comfortable seating. I myself have brought in cushions, couches (resource permitting) to session rooms

to make the room more comfortable for people.
- For remote sessions: Ensure clear instructions and technical support are available.

Example: Send an email with instructions for joining the session and troubleshooting tips for common technical problems.

Moderation Techniques

1. Be Neutral and Unbiased

Avoid leading participants or influencing their responses. Use open-ended questions like:

- "Can you describe your thought process as you complete this task?"
- "What are you expecting to happen next?"
- "Tell me about the last time you did something like this? "
- "Show me how you went about doing that task"

These "tell me more" and "show me how"

questions do wonders in opening up a conversation that might otherwise not happen if you asked a closed-ended question.

Avoid:

- “Do you think this button looks confusing?” Instead, ask - What are your thoughts on how you completed the task
- “Do you like this flow?” Instead, ask - what do you think about this flow?

Tip: Read about open ended research questions online.

3. Manage the Session Flow

Keep the session on track without rushing participants:

Start with an Introduction: Briefly explain the purpose of the session, assure participants there are no right or wrong answers, and emphasize that their feedback is valuable. Guide the Tasks: Clearly explain each task, but allow participants to explore freely.

There are going to be several times during a session when a participant will start talking about something that you are either not interested in or that feedback does not fulfill your research goals. Since time is of the essence in these sessions, make sure to find the appropriate moment, interject, acknowledge their feedback and bring them back to the topic of your interest.

Example: Imagine trying to interview someone how they purchased shoes online because you work at a retail company. Your goal is to find out problems people had when buying shoes on your website. However, in that conversation, the participant goes off on a tangent and says something along the lines of "Yeah last time I was buying shoes it was awesome. I purchased the perfect pair I wanted and also saw this wedding dress that was recommended to me. I know my friend was about to get married and was looking for a wedding dress so I started sharing some links to her and we got into a conversation about wedding dresses. We then made an appointment at this dress store ...." This is a very realistic scenario that might happen in your own study. Since the goal of your study

was to study their experience with shoe shopping, all the feedback about dresses is not really relevant. Find a moment and interject in a way that is respectful. Something like "Hey that's so great to hear and thank you for sharing that with me. I do however have to respect your limited time you have with us and would like to go back to how you went about finding that perfect pair of shoes you were talking about"
Wrap Up: Thank participants, summarize key points, and invite additional comments.

4. Handle Silence Strategically

Silence can encourage participants to share their thoughts without feeling rushed. If a participant seems stuck, offer gentle guidance.

Example: If they hesitate, ask, "What are you thinking right now?". Silence, while awkward in a conversation, does wonders in getting you rich feedback from the participants. It gives them a moment to think and then articulate in a richer way or add more context in what they might have just said. Try this yourself in a study. After a participant answers your question, don't feel rushed to acknowledge or say something. Just stay quiet for 3-5 seconds. Yes that'll be awkward but you'll notice that they would almost always follow up and add more to their feedback. Of course, using this technique after every question is not recommended so think strategically about questions upfront where you want rich feedback and then apply it.

5. Adapt to Participants

Every participant is different. Be flexible and adjust your approach based on their behavior. You might encounter participants that are not that upfront about feedback where you'd have to use encouragement to help them feel at ease. On the other hand, as mentioned above, you might run into talkative participants where you will have to politely redirect the conversation to stay focused. In one of my studies I was conducting, the participant was an 18 year old and we had to go to her house for an ethnographic study. I had several team members with me there to listen to the conversation. Right after starting the interview, I could tell that she was nervous seeing all these new faces in her house and wasn't very forthcoming or articulate in her responses because of that. Seeing that, I had to let go of the study for a moment and focus on making her feel comfortable. I started a random conversation with her about a fluffy bear that was kept on a desk behind her and asked her to tell me that story on how she got it. She started telling me that story and in the process loosened up and became much more comfortable at which point I eased back into the study.

Making participants at ease is one of the most important goals before starting the study. You'll have to be aware of how the participant is feeling and adapt to that environment pretty fast. This is one of the reasons why Empathy as one of the skills of a UX Researcher is so important and comes in handy during situations like these.

Ethical Considerations in UX Research

1. Obtain Informed Consent

Ensure participants understand the study's purpose and their rights.

- Provide a Consent Form: Include details about the session, how data will be used, and confidentiality assurances.
- Explain Clearly: Verbally explain the consent process before starting.

2. Respect Privacy

1. Protect participants' personal information by:

- Anonymizing data in reports.
- Storing data securely to prevent unauthorized access. Avoiding unnecessary collection of sensitive information.
- Example: Use pseudonyms or participant IDs in research findings.

2. Avoid Harm or Discomfort

- Design sessions to minimize any potential stress or discomfort:
- Be patient and supportive if participants struggle.
- Allow participants to skip questions or tasks they find uncomfortable.

- Offer breaks during longer sessions.

3. Be Transparent

Inform participants if the session is being recorded. Share how their feedback will contribute to the project. Answer any questions they may have about the research.

4. Provide Compensation Fairly

Ensure compensation is appropriate and delivered promptly, as agreed upon during recruitment.

5. Adhere to Ethical Guidelines

Follow established UX research ethical standards, such as those outlined by the American Psychological Association (APA) or other relevant organizations.

Sample interview guide

Here is an example of what an interview guide might look like for a UX Researcher working on a checkout flow for a retail website.

Introduction (5 minutes)

- Warmly greet the participants and thank them for their time.
- Briefly introduce yourself and your role.
- Explain the purpose of the study: to understand their experiences and challenges with online checkout processes.
- Emphasize that there are no right or wrong answers, and their honest feedback is valuable.
- Obtain consent to audio record the session (if applicable).
- Remind them their responses will be kept confidential.

Thank you for taking the time today to attend this session. My name is [x] and I am the UX Researcher working on this project. The purpose of our limited time together today is for us to understand how you shop online and what do you like about it or dislike. My role today is to sit and learn as much as possible from you and how you go about shopping online. There are no right or wrong answers and I simply want to listen and understand.

Warm-up Questions (5 minutes)

- Tell me a little bit about yourself and your online shopping habits.
- What types of websites or apps do you typically shop on?
- How often do you make purchases online?
- What are some of your favorite online retailers and why?

Checkout Flow Exploration (20 minutes)

- **Scenario:** Imagine you're about to purchase [product relevant to the study] online. Walk me through the steps you would take from browsing to completing the order.
- **Think-aloud:** As you go through the process, please verbalize your thoughts, feelings, and any questions that arise.
- **Probing Questions:**
    - What are your preferred payment methods? Why?
    - Have you ever abandoned an online order during checkout? If so, why?

    - What are your biggest frustrations or concerns when checking out online?
    - What could make the checkout process easier or more enjoyable for you?
    - Are there any features or functionalities you wish were included in the checkout process?
    - How important are factors like shipping costs, delivery time, and return policy to you?
    - Do you have any security concerns when entering personal or payment information online?

Specific Feature Deep Dive (10 minutes)

- **[Feature 1, e.g., Guest Checkout]:**
    - How do you feel about the option to checkout as a guest?
    - Do you typically create an account or use guest checkout? Why?
    - What are the advantages and disadvantages of each option in your opinion?

- **[Feature 2, e.g., Progress Indicator]:**
    - How helpful is it to have a visual progress indicator during checkout?
    - Would you prefer a different way of displaying progress?
- **[Feature 3, e.g., Form Fields]:**
    - Are there any fields in the checkout form that you find unnecessary or confusing?
    - How could the form be improved to be more user-friendly?

Wrap-up (5 minutes)

- Thank the participants for their time and valuable feedback.
- Answer any questions they may have about the study.
- Provide any incentives promised (if applicable).
- Leave the participant with a positive impression of the research process.

Note:

- This is a sample interview guide and should be adapted based on the specific goals and scope of your research study.

- You can adjust the time allocated to each section as needed.
- It's important to be flexible and allow the conversation to flow naturally, while still ensuring you cover the key areas of interest.
- Remember to actively listen, observe non-verbal cues, and probe for deeper insights.

Conclusion

Conducting UX research requires careful preparation, skilled moderation, and strict adherence to ethical standards. By creating a well-structured session, moderating thoughtfully, and respecting participants' rights, you ensure the process yields actionable and trustworthy insights.

In the next chapter, we'll explore how to analyze and interpret the data collected from research sessions to uncover meaningful patterns and insights.

CHAPTER 9:

ANALYZING & INTERPRETING DATA

After conducting UX research, the next step is to analyze the data and transform it into actionable insights. Effective analysis ensures your findings are grounded in evidence and aligned with your research goals. This chapter explores techniques for analyzing qualitative and quantitative data, and strategies for identifying patterns and drawing meaningful insights.

Qualitative Data Analysis

What is Qualitative Data?

Qualitative data includes non-numerical information, such as user feedback, interview transcripts, and observational notes. It's rich in context and helps explain the "why" behind user behaviors.

Steps for Analyzing Qualitative Data

- Organize Your Data:
    - Collect all qualitative data in one place.
    - Notes from usability testing sessions.
    - Observational data from contextual inquiries.

  Different people have different preferences for note taking during the sessions. Some people like to do it in documents while others like spreadsheets. I personally am biased towards spreadsheets as it allows me to look at data from across participants in one place but please choose the method to your liking.

- Familiarize Yourself with the Data:
    - Read the data multiple times to gain a comprehensive understanding. Highlight interesting quotes, recurring

themes, or surprising observations.

- Code the Data:
    - Assign labels (codes) to specific pieces of data based on recurring themes or categories.
    - Example: For feedback on an e-commerce app:
    - “Easy to navigate” → Positive usability.
    - “Couldn’t find the search bar” → Navigation issue.

- Group Codes into Themes:
    - Combine related codes to identify overarching themes.
    - Example Themes:
    - Navigation challenges.
    - Satisfaction with product search.

- Synthesize Insights:
    - Look at the themes to draw conclusions about user behavior, preferences, and pain points.
    - Example: In a usability test for a

travel booking site, users frequently comment on difficulties with the search filters. Coding reveals themes like:

- Confusion over filter terminology.
- Desire for multi-select options.
- Insight: Simplifying filter labels and adding multi-select functionality can improve the experience.

No solution without a problem

Before we go further I want to spend some time talking about the importance of problem identification. While everyone understands how important finding a problem is it is harder for people to truly connect a solution to a problem. People's intentions are always right that they want to do research and they do it perfectly but then fail to integrate research findings into solution design. This results in several challenges

- The solutions that are then created are done in a vacuum without any problems attached to it that make them more likely to fail
- While everyone says that they have done research, that research goes to waste as it is not connected to the solutions.

Here are some examples. Read through the problem and solution statements below and think about what's wrong in that.

Problem Statement 1: Many students struggle to stay focused during online lectures, leading to decreased information retention and lower grades.

Solution Statement 1: A new app will be developed that utilizes facial recognition technology to track user engagement during virtual meetings. This app will send automated reminders to participants to take breaks and stretch, aiming to improve overall well-being.

Problem Statement 2: The rising cost of

ingredients and supplies is making it difficult for small, independent bakeries to compete with larger chain stores, leading to potential closures and a decline in the variety of baked goods available to consumers.

Solution Statement 2: A new program will be launched to install solar panels on the rooftops of community centers across the city. This initiative aims to reduce energy costs for public buildings, freeing up funds for other community improvement projects.

As you can see, while the problem statement from research exists, the solution that ends up getting created is disconnected from it. So while people can say that yes they did research and followed the UCD process, it almost does not matter because they failed to connect the problem to the solution, making the solution less useful or usable to people it was designed for.

Why does that happen?

The reason a solution gets disconnected from the problem (and should be avoided) is for the following reasons

1. Mis-diagnosis of the problem - Research was done but the UX Researcher failed to deeply understand why the problem was happening leading to its misdiagnosis. One reason this can often happen is not asking "why" in interviews to deeply understand the user point of view.
2. Jumping to solutions quickly - People did not spend enough time in understanding or creating user insights and jumped to designing and solution creation.
3. Confirmation bias - Doing research was just a checkbox to check because the team had their own confirmation bias and "knew" along what to build. This led to research that did not get used in creating solutions.
4. External pressures - There were dependencies and pressures from up top, competitors, resource wise etc that did not allow the team to spend time in understanding user insights leading to solutions being created in a vacuum.

There are many adverse implications when solutions get created in a vacuum. Wasted research work, wasted product development work as we find issues much later, low adoption of the product since users don't find value in the solutions that got built and many more.

So, how do we connect solutions to problems?

The end outcome is that insights we create end up being tied to solutions. But that is not where it starts. Going back to the research process outlined in chapter 4, it all starts with the research questions.

Your research questions define your interview guide. The interview guide has to be set up in a way that you are asking "why" questions to understand the underlying needs and motivations. The responses you collected from that interview guide go into your note taking doc which then becomes the source from where you start your research synthesis to identify problems once the study is complete.

The emphasis I made on planning your research is something I want to re-emphasize at this point that it all starts at the beginning. The quality of insights and the problems you define during synthesis start at the very beginning when you define your goals and research questions.

So to answer the question around how we connect solutions to problems is threefold

1) Plan your research well that ultimately allows you to take good notes
2) Follow a good research synthesis approach (described below) that allows you to find patterns and insights
3) Use the insights to create "how might we" statements that then inform solutions. (Chapter 10)

Outcomes from a Research synthesis

In the process of research synthesis, there are some common outcomes you can hope to achieve. While looking at the raw data you have collected, you are trying to understand and differentiate between user needs, behaviors, pain points, tools they use etc. It is important to have a proactive coding model developed before you start your synthesis process. Some common codes could be the following

- Goal: What the person is trying to accomplish as an outcome.
- Need: Something a person needs to fulfill a goal.
- Motivation: Why the person is trying to achieve that goal.
- Task: Something a person does to achieve a goal.
- Pain point: A barrier or difficulty towards accomplishing a goal.
- Tools: A tool a person uses to try to accomplish a goal.

Let's go through a prompt around "Design an

app that helps people discover new TV shows". This is also very often a style of interview question you are given by companies. The trap here is that even though the question asks you to "design", always remember that any solution you build has to be tied to a problem. Since the problem hasn't yet been defined, always start your response by outlining a research process that'll help you identify the problem first before jumping to a solution or design.

If you are the UX Researcher for the above prompt, going back to the research process, you'd start with a generative style interviewing approach to understand people's needs and behaviors and write up a research plan that outlines goals and questions. Let's imagine you come up with the following questions

Awareness:

- What are people's preferred sources for finding out about new TV shows
- How much time do people typically dedicate to actively searching for new shows?
- What factors influence people's

openness to trying new TV shows

Consideration:

- What information do people find most helpful when deciding whether to watch a new TV show
- How do people typically evaluate whether a new TV show is a good fit for them
- Do people rely on recommendations from friends or family, and if so, what makes those recommendations trustworthy?

Decision:

- Where do people typically go to watch new TV shows once they've decided on one
- What factors influence the platform people choose to watch a new show on
- Do people ever abandon a new show after starting it, and if so, what are the most common reasons

Experience:

- How do people typically discover new episodes of shows they're already watching

- What features or functionalities on streaming platforms do people find most helpful when watching TV shows
- Do people discuss the TV shows they're watching with others, and if so, on what platforms

For one of your questions, the participant responds something like the following

“First and foremost, the genre has to be something I'm interested in. I also like to read the synopsis or watch the trailer to get a sense of the overall premise. If it sounds intriguing and like something I'd enjoy the story unfolding, that's a good sign.I'll usually skim through some reviews and user ratings to get a general feel for the show. While I don't want spoilers, I do want to know if the overall reception is positive and if the show seems well-made.These days, my time is precious. I tend to avoid shows with super long episodes, especially if it's a new series I'm unsure about. Knowing the episode length helps me gauge the time commitment involved.If there are actors or creators I know and enjoy their work, that definitely makes me more likely to give a show a try. Familiar faces or names associated with quality projects can be a deciding factor. I might watch a trailer or some clips to get a sense of the show's visual style. If the cinematography, editing, or overall aesthetic appeals to me, it makes the show more inviting."

This is a sample response for one of the many questions you would ask participants. So if you end up talking to 8 people and have 10-15 questions to ask, you can do the math on how much data you have at this point.

With the coding mechanism described above, the challenge becomes how do you tease out those aspects from this response. What we're looking for in this raw data is what is a need, what is a motivation, what is a problem etc.

Need:

- In the excerpt above, when the participant says "the genre has to be something I'm interested in" shows us that one of the user needs is seeing content that is relevant.

- When the participant says "Overall reception is positive" it shows us that the other user need is social validation

Pain point

- When the participant says "While I don't want spoilers" it shows us that maybe they have encountered experiences where they might have seen spoilers which was a pain point for them.

Behaviors

- When the participant says "I might watch a trailer" it is a behaviour they have while assessing TV shows

You get the point by now. By slowly and steadily going through the raw responses we can start teasing apart the responses and code them. It gives you a systematic way to start making sense of the raw data. Coding the data allows us to now start thinking about how to frame insights and start writing up a report. Reminder: An insight is What + Why and is basically a sentence written by the UX Researcher to outline a human behavior, pain point or need.

When you look at the above raw data, a potential insight that could be written is

“Users had a need for quality TV shows without revelation of plot details and found rating systems or curated user reviews to be helpful”

Another one from the data above that could be written is

“Clearly display the average episode length alongside show descriptions. This empowers users to make informed choices about time commitment, especially for new shows they're unsure about”

While the raw data could look overwhelming to begin with, structuring the data with good coding, eliminating what is not needed and then framing insights by combining needs, motivations and behaviors makes it much more manageable and allows you to sensemake it.

Another aspect that'll come in handy here is the decisions you knew about that your study was going to inform. Since you had that information and you collected data around that, you know what information to synthesize for your findings that can help alleviate some of the overwhelming nature of the raw data.

A word on "Why"

A critical point to note here is to think about how to even come up with the data in your interview in the first place that can then be coded. To code the data across those categories, you have to have it in the first place. That is where the importance of asking "why" comes in. When you start talking to a participant about any question, they would very often start responding with the "What". Try this on your friend and ask them "how do you spend your day?". The first set of responses they'd give you is what they do. Now while that is important, it is really hard to design solutions around the what because that *what* has a huge range of diversity when you go from one person to another person. Someone might tell you that they start their day by brushing their teeth and getting ready for work while others could tell you that they start their day by getting their kids school lunch ready. As you can see just from this there is no need or motivation or pain point that is captured from those responses. This is where "why" comes in. Follow up on those whats they have told you and ask why they do things the way they do. Asking why questions helps uncover the underlying needs and motivations people have which is where you will start to find similarities across participants. E.g. The person who gets ready first to start their day might be doing so to save time for their commute to work while the person preparing kids lunch might be doing it to save time as their work meetings start early. This insight could only be uncovered by asking why after the what they just told you. Now since you know the motivation behind both these different whats is the same why (save time) your solution can now cater to that common need.

Designs and solutions are better created when we know the motivation and the underlying need behind what people do which is why it is imperative to always ask why in your interviews. Without why, the coding above won't be possible and your raw data will look like a huge collection of disjointed whats.

Quantitative Data Analysis

What is Quantitative Data?

Quantitative data is numerical and can be measured and analyzed statistically. It includes metrics like task completion rates, survey ratings, or click-through rates

Steps for Analyzing Quantitative Data

- Clean Your Data: Check for incomplete responses, duplicates, or errors. Remove any irrelevant data points.
- Choose Descriptive Statistics:
    - Use basic statistics to summarize your data:
    - Mean: Average value (e.g., average task completion time).
    - Median: Middle value in a data set (useful for skewed data).
    - Mode: Most frequently occurring value.

- Visualize the Data:
    - Create charts or graphs to make the data easier to interpret: Bar Charts:
    - Compare categories (e.g., satisfaction ratings).
    - Line Graphs: Show trends over time (e.g., user engagement rates).
    - Heatmaps: Visualize click patterns on a webpage.
- Run Statistical Tests (If Needed):
    - If comparing groups, use statistical tests to validate findings:
    - A/B Testing: Compare performance metrics for two versions of a design.
    - T-Tests or ANOVA: Test differences between multiple groups.
- Interpret Results:
    - Focus on actionable insights, not just raw numbers.

Identifying Patterns and Insights

Identifying patterns involves linking findings across qualitative and quantitative data to uncover deeper insights.

Techniques for Identifying Patterns

- Look for Recurring Themes:
    - Identify consistent feedback or behaviors across different participants or data sources.
    - Example: In usability testing, 7/8 participants struggle with the same feature, highlighting a critical usability issue.

- Combine Data Types:
    - Use qualitative insights to explain quantitative trends. Example: A low task completion rate (quantitative) aligns with user comments about confusing navigation (qualitative).

- Use Affinity Diagrams:
    - Group related pieces of data on sticky notes or a digital tool to

visualize connections and categorize themes.

- Prioritize Findings:
    - Use frameworks like the Impact vs. Effort Matrix to determine which issues to address first.
    - High Impact, Low Effort: Quick wins, such as fixing minor usability issues.
    - High Impact, High Effort: Major improvements requiring substantial resources.

Example Scenario: Analyzing Research Data

- Scenario: A UX team conducts research for a new budgeting app.
- Qualitative Findings: Users frequently mention that graphs are hard to read. Many users struggle to locate their transaction history.
- Quantitative Findings: Task completion rate: 60% (users locating transaction history). Average satisfaction score: 3.5/5.
- Patterns Identified: Poor visibility of the transaction history feature contributes to low task completion

rates. Simplifying graph designs could improve satisfaction scores.

- Insights: Redesign the navigation to make transaction history easier to find.
- Use cleaner, more legible graphs to enhance data visualization.

As much as possible, aim to design your research to uncover both the what and the why in as much richness as possible. It'll allow you to then triangulate findings and put forward a more confident and complete insight.

Tips for Effective Analysis

- Focus on Research Goals: Revisit your original objectives to ensure findings align with the purpose of the study.

- Collaborate with Your Team: Involve designers, developers, and partners in the analysis process to gain diverse perspectives. Remember, collaboration and relationship building is key to the role of UX Researchers

- Focus on decisions: Go back to your

research plan to see what decisions this research was going to inform and create outcomes that help inform them.

Conclusion

Analyzing and interpreting data is where raw research transforms into actionable insights. Whether working with qualitative or quantitative data, the key lies in organizing, synthesizing, and connecting findings to identify meaningful patterns. This process enables you to make informed decisions that enhance user experiences and meet business objectives.

In the next chapter, we'll discuss how to present your findings effectively to partners and teams, ensuring your insights drive meaningful change.

CHAPTER 10:

PRESENTING YOUR FINDINGS

Conducting research is only half the battle. The real impact comes from effectively presenting your findings. A well-crafted presentation ensures that partners understand the insights and feel empowered to act. This chapter will guide you through creating engaging reports, visualizing data effectively, and delivering actionable recommendations.

Creating Engaging Reports

An engaging research report doesn't just summarize data—it tells a story. It connects user insights to business goals and design decisions.

I won't delve into the basic structure of a research presentation as that is pretty well known, but I will talk about some salient aspects that people get to know when they enter the industry.

Executive Summary:

A concise overview of key findings, methods, and recommendations. When partners come into a research presentation meeting, they are often running from one meeting to another and are often 3-5 minutes late. They are of the mindset that we did a bunch of work on this project and now want to hear what we found so they can start making changes. Traditionally, UX Research presentations have shied away from jumping right into the findings and give a walk through of the goals, methods, sample etc which take up 4-8 slides and probably 10 minutes in the meeting.

I have seen that effective research presentations are the ones that dive right in the findings and start giving out punchy insights. I am not saying that sharing the methodology, goals and sample and other context is not important but more often than not I have found that those details are something people are already aware of and starting with those in a presentation often takes up valuable time and attention. Starting with those makes people lose interest and get them to start browsing on their laptops. Having a title slide in the beginning and getting right into the insights gets them interested and produces active discussion in the meeting.

- Findings: Key insights organized by themes or research questions. Combine qualitative quotes with quantitative data for depth.
- Recommendations: Actionable suggestions linked to specific findings. Prioritize recommendations based on impact and feasibility.
- Appendices (if needed):
    - Method
    - Research objectives and questions.
    - Scope of the study.
    - Participant criteria
    - Detailed data tables.
    - Research instruments (e.g.,

survey questions).
    - Raw transcripts or session notes.

Writing Tips for Reports

- Be Concise: Avoid unnecessary jargon or lengthy explanations.
- Use Storytelling: Present insights in a narrative that resonates with your audience. Readers often skim through the presentation when going through it by themselves. One way to think about storytelling is to write slide headings in a way that one heading connects to the heading on the next slide like in a paragraph. So if someone only reads the headings while skimming the presentation, they still walk out of the deck with a story in mind. This is also a good self-check to flip the slides and read the title and see if your presentation is telling a story.
- Highlight Impact: Connect findings to potential user and business outcomes.
- Try coming up with visualizations for

otherwise textual insights. Use charts, diagrams, flows etc to illustrate what you're trying to say in a text form
- Connect recommendations to business outcomes: Insights alone are not enough; partners need clear, actionable steps to improve the product.

Characteristics of Actionable Recommendations

- Specific:
    - Clearly define what should be done.
    - Example: "Reduce the number of steps in the checkout process from five to three."
- Evidence-Based:
    - Link recommendations to research findings.
    - Example: "Users expressed frustration with long forms, contributing to a 40% drop-off rate during checkout."
- Prioritized:
    - Rank recommendations based

on impact and effort. Example Framework: High impact, low effort tasks should be addressed first. There is always a lot of work to do in industries and what the team is looking for is the top 3-5 biggest problems they should solve now considering engineering constraints.

- Aligned with Goals:
    - Ensure recommendations align with business and user objectives.

Tip: Read the book “Leading executive conversations” by Sally Williamson

Conclusion

Presenting UX research findings is a crucial step in driving user centered design. By creating engaging reports, visualizing data effectively, and delivering actionable recommendations, you ensure your insights lead to meaningful improvements. In the next chapter, we’ll explore how to integrate research findings into the design process, ensuring a seamless transition from insight to implementation.

CHAPTER 11:

INTEGRATING RESEARCH INTO DESIGN

Collecting insights from UX research is only valuable if they lead to meaningful changes in design. Remember from the first chapter that UX Researchers are accountable for not just doing research but also to make sure that their research impacts the product. Integrating research into the design process requires close collaboration with designers and developers, iterative testing to refine solutions, and measuring the impact of implemented changes. Here again, re-emphasizing how collaboration and relationship building becomes important. This chapter explores these critical aspects of bridging research with design.

Collaborating with Designers and Developers

Why Collaboration Matters

Effective collaboration ensures that research insights are translated into actionable design and development decisions. When researchers, designers, and developers work together, they create user-centered solutions that align with technical feasibility and business goals.

Best Practices for Collaboration

The one and only tip I'd give you here is to involve your partners early and keep them involved throughout the research process. Share with them your research plan, ask for feedback, set up meetings to align on goals and metrics, ensure everyone is aware and aligned on what the study is going to accomplish and not accomplish. Keep them involved when the study is happening by inviting them to sessions, think about ways to synthesize data together etc. I'd keep repeating this throughout the book that the more inclusive and collaborative your research is the more likelihood of it creating impact.

Another aspect of integrating research into design is to collaborate with your partners to help them translate your research findings into design decisions. E.g. If your research insight says "People were confused about what payment methods they can use during the checkout process because they couldn't find the options available", ask your designer if they have enough information from this insight to design the solution or if not, what are they missing and how can you help bridge that gap. The insights might seem obvious to us but might not for everyone. Work with your team to ensure these insights are translated into decisions that can help move the product forward.

A common way to do that is to host a "How might we" workshop. It is essentially a workshop with the partners where UX Researchers present user problems and insights and for each insight the team writes a How might we statement to hypothesize solutions to solve the problem.

E.g. for the problem “People were confused about what payment methods they can use during the checkout process because they couldn’t find the options available” corresponding “how might we” could be “How might we make the payment options more discoverable during the checkout process”.

User problem or insight	**How might we**
People were confused about what payment methods they can use during the checkout process because they couldn’t find the options available	How might we make the payment options more discoverable during the checkout process
People did not always want to enter their credit card number because it was cumbersome	How might we enable easy ways to allow users to enter their credit card details without

especially if it was not already saved in their profile	having to type it.

This approach has several benefits

1. It connects the solutions the team comes up with directly to user problems. This way the solutions end up solving a real user problem or a need as opposed to living on their own. (Don't build the ladder until you first find the wall.
2. It helps integrate research to design thereby showing impact.
3. It enables UX researchers to make sure that the insights are being translated into a form UX Designers can then use to design solutions and are not left to anyone's interpretation.
4. It brings the entire team on the same page around the problems, solutions and how they are connected together.

At the end, the workshop ends up creating several how might we's that are tied to user problems. Those how might we's are then taken by the designer to start creating solutions. Once the solutions are created, UX Researcher might go back to run evaluative research to see if the new designs solved the problems for the users or not.

Another way to integrate research insights into design is Iterative Design and Testing

What is Iterative Design?

Iterative design involves cycles of prototyping, testing, and refining a product based on user feedback. This approach ensures the design evolves with user needs and expectations.

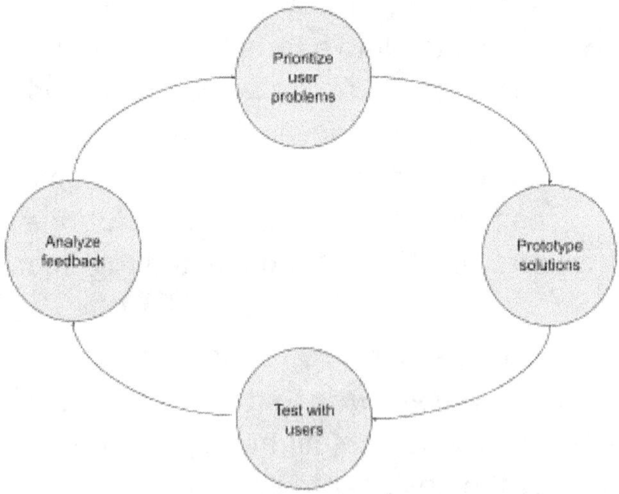

- Prototype: Create low-fidelity (e.g., wireframes) or high-fidelity (e.g., interactive) prototypes.Focus on specific features or workflows identified as pain points in research.
- Test with Users: Conduct usability tests or A/B testing to evaluate the prototype. Gather feedback on functionality, usability, and satisfaction.
- Analyze Feedback: Identify recurring issues or areas for improvement. Prioritize changes based on impact and feasibility.
- Refine and Repeat: Update the design based on findings and test again. Continue iterating until the design meets user needs effectively.

Benefits of Iterative Design

Iterate design approach reduces risk by addressing issues early. More importantly, because of the nature of the work, this process does wonders in building relationships and fostering collaboration by bringing the team together on a unified approach.

Example Scenario: Integrating Research into Design

- Context: A team is redesigning a fitness app to improve its onboarding process.
- Collaboration: Researchers share findings that users feel overwhelmed by too many setup questions. Designers propose a streamlined onboarding flow with fewer steps. Developers ensure technical feasibility and integrate analytics tracking.
- Iteration: Prototype a simpler onboarding process. Conduct usability tests to ensure users can complete the flow in under two minutes. Refine the design based on feedback, like adding progress indicators.
- Measuring Impact: Pre-redesign onboarding completion rate: 65%. Post-redesign onboarding completion rate: 92%. User satisfaction with

onboarding: 4.7/5 (up from 3.9/5).

- Outcome: The redesign enhances user engagement and reduces churn, showcasing the value of UX research.

Conclusion

Integrating research into design ensures that user insights drive meaningful improvements. By fostering collaboration, adopting iterative processes, and measuring the impact of changes, you create products that align with both user expectations and business goals. In the next chapter, we'll discuss common challenges in UX research and strategies for overcoming them, ensuring your research efforts remain effective and impactful.

CHAPTER 12:

COMMON CHALLENGES DURING TRANSITIONING TO INDUSTRY

While I have sprinkled industry examples throughout the book, I wanted to write a chapter to outline the biggest shifts I see when transitioning careers to an industry after school or during your first several years in a company. I hope this chapter helps you understand the context in which UX Researchers operate in a company, what the environment looks like and what tradeoffs people make.

Building relationships

I have spelled it out in the previous chapters but I'll say it here again. Building relationships is by far the most important aspect you will have to learn and internalize in your job as a UX Researcher when entering the industry. The reason it is the most important and why it often comes as a shock to people is because all of a sudden there is this new variable that comes into picture which we haven't been taught about how to manage - and that variable is People. People make decisions, drive conversations, provide constraints and the better you become in partners management and collaboration the better you will be at your job.

Almost every aspect of your job requires you to effectively collaborate with your partners in an inclusive environment. How you bring them along in the process of research takes time and effort but in the end it is completely worth it in making your research more impactful. It may seem counterintuitive, but academic training in research does not automatically translate to success in industry. While academia teaches research skills, it intentionally does not talk about the crucial aspect of partners management, which is vital in industry. This creates a steep learning curve for those transitioning from academia to industry, as they must learn to navigate partners relationships on their own, adding to the existing challenges.

I'll repeat some of the strategies I have outlined above to build relationships

1. **Set up a meeting cadence**: Meet with your partners weekly/biweekly to stay abreast of the priorities, keep them up to date on the research timeline, understand decisions that are being made, what work is being prioritized and what isn't. These meetings serve as a key way to build relationships and understand changes that are happening.
2. **Make research inclusive** - Involve partners in every part of your work as much as possible. Share with them your research goals, meet with them to get feedback, invite them to research sessions and readouts. Be transparent about the methods, what questions you are going to ask, send them pre-reads of your research

presentation etc. The more involved they are, the more it becomes everyone's work than just your work.

3. **Help bridge the gap between insight and decision** - Help them understand what user insights mean in terms of the changes that need to be made. The more you help them team bridge that gap, the more equipped they'll be in making those changes and will value your work even more.

Dealing with Limited Resources

Resources are defined as time, money and people. It is one of the most prominent challenges people face entering the industry. There is only so much time and only so many people to do the work required. As a result, while UX Researchers can have 10-15 recommendations ready to go out, realistically speaking, not all of them get implemented.

UX Researchers must adapt to this new mindset in all aspects of their work. Some examples

1. A UX Research plan is going to take 7 weeks to execute but the team needs results in 2 weeks for them to implement the changes.
2. A study that has to happen in a contextual environment in people's home/office can't happen anymore because team members who had to attend the study can't travel anymore.
3. The ideal study method is not possible anymore because the team does not have the budget to buy the software that was supposed to be used to analyze quantitative data
4. The UX Researcher came up with 10 very critical findings but the team can't implement them all as the engineers are tied up in other projects.

And so on.. This is to some extent, a day in the life of a UX Researcher. What is needed in these circumstances is creative thinking to overcome these constraints and without compromising the research integrity, thinking about ways to still deliver the results.

Strategies to Overcome Limited Resources

- Prioritize Research Goals:
    - Focus on the most critical questions that will have the greatest impact.
    - Use frameworks like the MoSCoW Method (Must-Have, Should-Have, Could-Have, Won't-Have) to prioritize research efforts.
    - Example: For a tight deadline, prioritize usability testing for high-risk features rather than conducting a full-scale survey.
    - This is also a very common interview question where an interviewer will ask you to design a research plan and ask a follow up question something like "What would you do if you only had a week instead of a month". This is their way of putting constraints on your plan and seeing how you adapt to those changes
- Prioritize recommendations

    - Knowing that the engineering team does not have the bandwidth to implement all the changes, go into your research presentation with a prioritization of what you think is most important to get fixed/built.
    - Since engineering teams have timelines/phases when that work happens, try to get the leftover recommendations in a future product release.

- Leverage Low-Cost Tools:

    - Use free or affordable tools for surveys, prototyping, and data analysis.
    - Examples: Google Forms, Figma, Miro, or Hotjar for basic analytics.

- Recruit Strategically:

    - Tap existing user bases or social media to find participants.

    - Offer non-monetary incentives like exclusive product previews or discounts.

- Adopt Guerrilla Research:

    - Conduct quick, informal studies in natural user environments, such as coffee shops or coworking spaces.
    - Example: Testing a new app interface by asking volunteers at a cafe for five minutes of their time.

Managing partners Expectations

In an industry setting, this is probably the most common issue you will run into and is very much tied to the "building relationships" point mentioned above. While collaboration is one of the most important aspects of UX Researcher's role in an industry it also has its fair share of challenges.

- Unrealistic Expectations: Expecting immediate, groundbreaking insights.
- Misalignment: Differing views on

research goals or scope.
- Limited Understanding of UX Research
- Underestimating the time, effort, or complexity involved.

Partners can have many expectations from your role or your work with some of them being incorrect or unrealistic. All the points mentioned below talk about relationship building to mitigate those unrealistic expectations.

Strategies to Manage Expectations

- Communicate Early and Often:
    - Set clear expectations for what research can and cannot achieve.
    - Provide a timeline with milestones to show progress.
    - Example: "This usability test will identify immediate usability issues, but it won't provide insights into long term engagement."

- Involve partners in the Process: As I

mentioned above, I'll keep repeating this point. The more collaborative and inclusive your research is, the more likelihood of it showing impact. Invite them to observe research sessions or attend workshops. Share preliminary findings during the research process to maintain transparency.

- Focus on Actionable Insights: Tie recommendations to business goals and user needs. Avoid overwhelming partners with excessive data and instead highlight the most impactful findings and what specifically the team should do about them. Don't leave the translation of insights into recommendations up to the team as much as it is possible.

Example Scenario: Overcoming Challenges

- Context: A small UX team is tasked with redesigning a website on a tight budget, facing conflicting feedback from users and partners.

- Dealing with Limited Resources: The team conducts guerrilla usability testing in a coworking space to gather quick insights. They use free tools like Figma for prototypes and Google Forms for surveys.

- Managing partners Expectations: Early meetings clarify that the redesign will focus on usability rather than a complete visual overhaul. partners observe usability tests, helping them understand user pain points directly.

- Addressing Conflicting Feedback: Users are split on the navigation style. The team segments feedback by user type. Frequent users prefer a minimalist menu, while infrequent users need more guidance. They design a hybrid solution: a minimalist menu with an optional help overlay.

- Outcome: The redesign improves usability while balancing the needs of different user groups and partners priorities.

Prioritization

In the first six months as a UX Researcher, your initial project will likely expand into multiple sub-projects as you delve deeper into the problem space and uncover new areas for investigation. Additionally, as you establish yourself as a reliable and valuable team member, partners may approach you directly with additional research requests or ad-hoc projects. This can easily lead to a situation where you're working long hours, including weekends, to manage the increased workload.

It's important to recognize that there will always be more work than can be realistically accomplished within a given timeframe. Companies and teams are often under-resourced, and there's a constant pressure to deliver results quickly. It's crucial to develop strong prioritization skills and regularly ask yourself, "Am I working on the most impactful tasks that align with the team's and company's goals?"

The transition from academia to industry can be particularly challenging in this regard. In academia, research is often self-directed, and you have more control over your schedule and priorities. In industry, you're juggling multiple projects with competing deadlines, managing expectations from various partners, and navigating the complexities of organizational dynamics. Effective prioritization becomes essential for managing these demands and ensuring that your work delivers the most value to the organization.

To navigate this effectively, you should proactively communicate with your manager and partners about your workload and capacity. Regularly discuss priorities and trade-offs, and be transparent about potential challenges or delays. By setting realistic expectations and managing workload proactively, you can avoid burnout and ensure that your research has the maximum impact on the product and user experience.

Why Prioritization Matters

- Limited Resources: Time, budget, and participant availability are finite.

Prioritizing ensures you focus on research that delivers the most impact.

- Strategic Alignment: Your research should ladder up to company goals. Prioritization helps align your efforts with what truly matters to the business. At any given point of time, all the work you are doing has to have a direct line to the company's or your team's most important priorities and that "most important" work has to be aligned with all your partners.
- Prioritizing your tasks and focusing on the most important items first is a strategy that yields multiple benefits. By tackling high-priority tasks, you can mitigate feelings of stress and overwhelm that often accompany a long to-do list. This, in turn, creates space for more effective and efficient work, as your mental energy is not scattered across numerous competing tasks. Additionally, the sense of accomplishment that comes from completing important tasks can boost your overall well-being and motivation, creating a positive feedback loop that

further enhances productivity.

- Well-being - You will realize in the long run as you grow in your career that well-being takes a prominent shape in your brain and becomes a huge priority. While you can enter the industry with a can-do-it-all attitude (which is not wrong) it often translates into longer working hours that have an effect on your personal life. By compartmentalizing your work life to the highest priority work you can take control back of your life and still deliver impactful research.
- Increased Impact: By focusing on high-priority projects, you maximize the influence your research has on product decisions.

Tips for New UX Researchers

- Don't be afraid to push back: If a research request lacks clarity or seems low-impact, ask questions and advocate for your time.
- Start small and build momentum: Tackle quick wins early on to demonstrate the value of your work.

- Learn to say "no" (gracefully): Overcommitting leads to burnout and compromises research quality.

Mastering the art of prioritization is essential for any UX researcher transitioning to industry. By strategically focusing your efforts, you'll deliver impactful research that drives product decisions and elevates your value within the organization.

Culture of Feedback

Transitioning from the world of academia to the UX industry can feel like stepping onto a different planet. While rigorous research and theoretical knowledge are valuable foundations, the industry demands a different approach – one where feedback is the lifeblood of your work.

In academia, feedback often comes in the form of peer reviews or grades on carefully crafted research papers. The timeline is extended, and the focus is primarily on in-depth analysis and theoretical validation.

The industry, however, operates at a faster pace. Feedback is constant, iterative, and comes from various sources – your team, partners, and most importantly, users. It's no longer about proving a hypothesis but about **creating user-centered designs that solve real-world problems.**

Why Feedback is Essential in UX

1. **Iteration and Improvement:** Feedback helps you refine your designs & research plans and ensure they meet user needs and business goals. It's a continuous cycle of learning and improvement.

2. **User-Centered Design:** Feedback from users is crucial for understanding their perspectives, pain points, and preferences. It allows you to create designs that are truly user-centered.

3. **Collaboration and Communication:** Feedback fosters open communication and collaboration within your team and with partners. It ensures everyone is aligned and working towards the

same goals.

4. **Validation and Confidence:** Receiving positive feedback can validate your design decisions and boost your confidence. Constructive criticism helps you identify areas for improvement and grow as a UX professional.

5. **Adaptability and Growth:** The UX landscape is constantly evolving. Feedback helps you stay agile, adapt to new trends and technologies, and continuously improve your skills.

Types of Feedback in the UX Industry

- **User Feedback:** Gathered through usability testing, surveys, A/B testing, and user interviews.
- **Peer Feedback:** Reviews and critiques from fellow designers and team members.
- **partners Feedback:** Input from clients, product managers, and other decision-makers.

Developing a Feedback Mindset

- **Be open to criticism:** View feedback as an opportunity to learn and grow, not a personal attack.
- **Actively seek feedback:** Don't wait for it to come to you. Ask for it from various sources and at different stages of the design process.
- **Listen actively and empathetically:** Pay attention to what others are saying, ask clarifying questions, and try to understand their perspective.
- **Give constructive feedback:** When providing feedback to others, be specific, actionable, and focus on the work, not the person.

Remember: Feedback is a gift. Embrace it, learn from it, and use it to become a better UX professional. By developing a strong feedback mindset, you'll be well-equipped to navigate the challenges and thrive in the dynamic world of UX design.

Acknowledge what you don't know

When you first enter any industry, there will inevitably be a vast amount of information that you are not familiar with. This could range from the specifics of the product you're working on, the dynamics of the partners you'll be interacting with, to the nuances of how things operate within your company.

I've personally observed that a significant amount of self-doubt that arises in newcomers stems from these unknowns. This lack of information can often lead to hesitation in your work and feelings of impostor syndrome, where you doubt your abilities. What exacerbates this situation is the tendency for people to internalize this hesitation and try to combat it on their own, which can cause a great deal of stress.

My primary piece of advice is to acknowledge what you don't know and be open about it with your colleagues and managers. The more you communicate your uncertainties and show vulnerability, the more understanding and support you'll receive from those around you. They can provide guidance, offer assistance, and share their own experiences, which can help you navigate the learning curve and build confidence in your role.

Remember that everyone starts somewhere, and it's perfectly normal to have gaps in your knowledge when you're new to an industry. By being transparent about what you don't know and actively seeking help, you can accelerate your learning, overcome self-doubt, and set yourself up for success in your new career.

Conclusion

Challenges are inevitable in UX research, but with strategic approaches, they can be managed effectively. By prioritizing resources, aligning with partners, and navigating conflicting feedback, you ensure your research remains impactful and drives user-centered design.

CHAPTER 13:

BUILDING A PORTFOLIO: TRANSFERABLE VS NON TRANSFERABLE SKILLS

A very common question I have gotten from students and early career professionals is what they should include in their portfolio. While everyone's work and experience is different and there are multiple templates out there about how to create your portfolio, I won't go into the elements of one. What I'd like to go into is how to make your work, which could be very different or not relevant to the company you are applying to, relevant to them. One of the fears I have heard is that I won't get a job in company x because I have not done any work relevant to that company. This chapter will attempt to bust that myth and give you a framework on how to talk about your work in a way that makes it relevant and transferable to companies.

The 2 problems in portfolios

Let's start with a simple design portfolio that I have seen been presented in many interviews. A designer or a researcher comes in and shows the design they have worked on or the research project they have led. They just focus on that one design or that research without explaining the entire story or the context behind it. For the sake of this argument, let's imagine you designed a water bottle that looked like this.

The portfolio will involve some of the talking points around the characteristics of the water bottle that went into designing it. Candidates will talk about how big the bottle is, what color it is, how it can be filled, what the branding looks like etc. The whole conversation revolves around the bottle.

But guess what - if you are applying in a product development company, designing the bottle is just a small piece of the work that company does. Companies have a whole user centered process on how they build, design and ship products, something like this below. A flavor of this process was also described in the UCD process in one of the previous chapters.

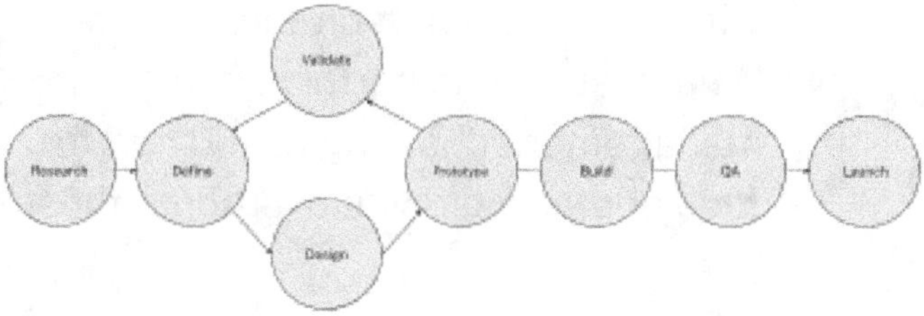

As you can see, Design is just one of the many steps companies or UX organizations take during product development. When portfolios focus heavily on the design itself, like the design of a bottle, they neglect to address the reasoning and process behind it. By showing and only talking about your output, you missed out on talking about how that design fit into the overall product development process. This leaves questions unanswered, such as the purpose of the design, the reasons behind specific design choices, alternative options explored, and partners management challenges. Some examples

- Why did you design the bottle in the first place? What was the problem that the bottle solves?
- Why is it green and not yellow or any other color?
- What other options did you come up with before landing on this design?
- What were some partners management challenges you had to face and how did you overcome those?
- ....

The focus on the final product rather than the thought process makes the work less relevant to companies outside the specific domain of the project. A successful portfolio communicates the designer's thought process and the intentionality behind the design, using the final product as a means of communication rather than the sole focus.

The second issue I find in portfolios is that candidates overly focus on their designs without explaining how their work is relevant to the companies they apply to. They don't differentiate between transferable and non-transferable skills. Non-transferable skills or work are projects done in school or for a previous employer, which are usually only transferable if applying to a company that does the same work. Transferable skills, like collaboration, communication, and prioritization, are built or learned while doing design or research work and can be transferred to any company.

Effective communication about your work during interviews is not to rely on one or the other but to intertwine your verbal and written communication to express both. Use transferable skills to outline your process and then give examples of how you have applied that process through a non-transferable skill. The ordering here is not important as one could go before the other but the essential thing is that we communicate both.

How to mitigate both the issues in your portfolio

I'll give a specific example of how to cover the entire product lifecycle and communicate transferable and non-transferable skills together. Let's walk through how you would talk about that bottle in a design portfolio communicating transferable and non-transferable skills.

Research phase: Always start with the research phase and talk about generative research you might have done that led to the solution of designing a bottle. You might say something like

- [Transferable skill] A process I normally follow when given a design project is that I always like to understand as a first step, what is the problem I am trying to solve. The problem comes from understanding our users and synthesizing data we gather before coming up with any solutions.

- [Non-transferable skill] Therefore in this project, I wanted to first understand what the problem is. I looked at past work, I talked to water bottle users, understood their pain points, what they like, dislike, why they use this brand's water bottle and no other.

As you can see, you communicated that it is a general practice of yours to identify the problem before coming up with a solution which is a transferable skill and can be applied to any sort of product development. It is important to know for employers and interviewers that you possess this skill and understanding but now they want to know have you done it before which is where the non-transferable skill comes in. By explaining the process of talking to this brand's users, you provided specific examples where you applied that skill and how you went about doing it.

Define phase: The define phase talks about data synthesis and definition of problems and needs identified from your research phase. Like in the previous phase, intertwine transferable and non-transferable skill in your communication something along the lines of

- [Transferable skill] We commonly synthesize research into needs, behaviors, problem statements etc to come up with insights. The synthesis process is often done with partners to get them invested in the work and get buy in upfront. The problem statements are then converted into HMWs to help start the design process

- [Non-transferable skill] And this is what we did in this project as well. I set up a synthesis workshop with the team where we collectively identified problems. Some of those were 1) The cap is too tight to open with one hand 2) The color is not appealing to all cultures 3) The Quantity of water is too much for people to drink in one go.

We converted these to HMWs to start designing

Are your interviewers only interested in the specific problems you found in the water bottle? Probably not. Are your interviewers only interested in knowing how you synthesize research? Yes but they want places where you have applied that theory. By combining transferable and non-transferable skills in your communication, you gave them a flavor of your skills (how you synthesize research) and then gave a specific example of how you have done that in a project.

I won't go into all the phases as you might get the point by now. By being in the thick of executing your school projects or work projects, you might now realize that you are working through a process but you are. It is just a matter of taking a step back and outlining it and communicating it.

Companies are not interested in just listening to the transferable skills as they alone sound too theoretical and they are not just interested in listening to non-transferable skills as they are not too relevant. By interweaving your response and presentation to include both gives them an idea of your thought process along with specific examples where you have applied that process. This way, even if your work has nothing to do with the company you are applying to, you can still make your skills appealing to potential employers. In the end, your communication looks somewhat like a heart wave that goes up and down talking about transferable and non-transferable skills.

Homework: Think about one of your own design projects and see how you would reframe your presentation content & talk about non-transferable and transferable skills.

Structure of a good portfolio presentation

Introduction (1-2 slides)

- **Who You Are:** Briefly introduce yourself and your background.

Highlight your passion for UX and your relevant skills (e.g., research methods, analytical thinking, communication).

- **Why UX?** Briefly explain your transition from academia to UX. Emphasize transferable skills and your enthusiasm for user-centered design.
- **Portfolio Overview:** Give a high-level overview of the projects you'll be presenting. Briefly mention the types of projects and the skills they demonstrate.
- **Your research process** - This is a good place to talk about the transferable skills and outline a generalized process you follow while approaching any research projects. Remember, the interviewers are in search of candidates who can fit the role they are hiring for and that work could be vastly different from what you are presenting. By laying out a standardized UX Process you can effectively communicate your approach and through case studies (below) talk about how you have applied or made tradeoffs on that process.

Project Case Studies

- **Project Context:**
- **The Problem:** Clearly define the problem or opportunity the project addressed. Connect it to a business goal (e.g., increase engagement, improve conversion). Talk about how difficult or complex the problem was in terms of partners management, product complexity, etc. You want to be able to explain the problem space to an extent that the listeners not only understand it but also to some extent empathize with it.
    - **Your Role:** Describe your specific role and responsibilities in the project. This is key - clearly explain your unique contributions in the project, what you did, what were you responsible for.

- **The Team:** If applicable, briefly mention who you collaborated with (e.g., designers, product managers). Again, collaboration is key in industry. Talk about who you collaborated with and how.

- **Research Process:**
  - **Methods:** Describe the research methods you used (e.g., user interviews, usability testing, surveys).
  - **Key Activities:** Highlight key activities like participant recruitment, data analysis, and synthesis.
  - **Visuals:** Use visuals (photos, diagrams, graphs) to illustrate your process and make the presentation more engaging.

- **Key Findings & Insights:**

    - **Focus on Impact:** Present your findings in a way that highlights their impact on the project and the business. Quantify your results whenever possible (e.g., "Usability testing revealed that 80% of users failed to complete the checkout process due to a confusing form").

- **Recommendations & Outcomes:**

    - **Actionable Recommendations:** Clearly articulate your recommendations based on your research.

    - **Show Impact:** Explain how your recommendations were implemented and what the outcomes were (e.g., "Based on my findings, the design team redesigned the form, resulting in a 15% increase in conversions").

3. Bridging the Gap: Highlighting Transferable Skills (1-2 slides)

- **Academic Research Skills:** Explicitly link your academic research experience to UX skills.
- **Examples:**
    - "My experience conducting literature reviews honed my ability to synthesize complex information and identify key insights."
    - "My background in qualitative research gave me a strong foundation in conducting user interviews and analyzing qualitative data."
    - "Presenting my research at academic conferences developed my communication and presentation skills, which are essential for effectively sharing UX findings with partners."

- **Adaptability and Learning:** Emphasize your ability to adapt to new environments and learn quickly. Highlight any steps you've taken to develop your UX skills (e.g., online courses, workshops, personal projects). Companies are looking for people who have a willingness to grow and learn and highlighting this area can go a long way in communicating that.

Decision intentionality

When delivering your presentation, it's crucial to incorporate the reasoning behind your decisions. It's equally important to elucidate not only your methods and processes but also the rationale behind those specific choices. This offers valuable insight into your decision-making process and how you navigate trade-offs when circumstances shift.

For instance, when elaborating on your research methods, articulate why you selected them. You could state, "Given the research questions, there were a few suitable methods, but I opted for a usability study due to time and resource constraints." Additionally, you could delve deeper into the trade-offs you considered, such as, "While a longitudinal study could have provided richer data, the time frame of the project necessitated a more rapid approach, making a usability study the optimal choice."

Explaining your rationale in this manner demonstrates intentionality and strategic thinking behind your decisions. This highlights your transferable skills, such as problem-solving, critical thinking, and adaptability. By connecting your choices to the constraints and objectives of the project, you showcase your ability to make informed decisions under pressure and effectively manage resources.

Furthermore, providing context for your decisions allows the audience to understand your thought process and appreciate the complexities involved in your work. This can lead to more engaging and insightful discussions, as it encourages the audience to ask questions and explore alternative approaches.

Remember, the goal is not just to showcase your accomplishments but also to demonstrate your ability to learn, adapt, and overcome challenges. By sharing your decision-making process and the rationale behind your choices, you paint a more complete picture of your skills and potential.

A good way to check if you have this in your portfolio is to go back and try to answer the question for yourself at each stage of the UX Research project you did and say

- "Why did I do it this way"
- "What other options did I have"?
- "What were the pros/cons of other approaches"

CHAPTER 14:

CASE STUDIES

In this chapter I wanted to outline a couple of case studies to show how a business problem translates into a UX Research goal and what a day in the life looks like for a UX Researcher working in a company.

Case study 1: High churn rate in an app

A popular app was experiencing high churn rates within the first week of use. The team hypothesized that users were struggling to understand the app's features and weren't seeing value quickly enough. A UX researcher working on the app was tasked with investigating what is going on and what product improvements could be made to mitigate this churn.

Setting the scene

Typically what happens in industries is when an insight comes to light, a UX Researcher is already in a meeting where this is being discussed or if not, the team members bring this to the person. Seeing that there is an opportunity for research to investigate why this might be happening the UX Researcher starts putting together a research plan.

Research Goals:

- Identify pain points and areas of confusion in the current onboarding process.
- Understand users' expectations and motivations for using the app.
- Develop recommendations for improving the onboarding experience to increase user engagement and retention.

Research Process:

The UX Researcher employed a mixed-methods approach:

- **User Interviews:** Conducted interviews with new users to understand their first impressions of the app, their goals for learning a language, and their frustrations with the onboarding process.

- **Usability Testing:** Observed users as they navigated through the onboarding flow, noting any areas where they struggled or got confused.
- **A/B Testing:** Tested different versions of the onboarding experience (e.g., varying the length, content, and interactive elements) to see which led to higher user engagement and retention.

Decisions to be made:

- If we knew that the value proposition of the app is not coming across, we will refine the text to communicate that more clearly
- If we knew there are usability problems with the onboarding flow, we will prioritize to fix them in the upcoming release

Participant criteria

1. People who have already used the app but left within a week (higher priority)
2. People who have never used the app

Collaboration: Since UX Research is a highly collaborative activity, at this time the researcher will send out this plan to their partners in a doc or share in a meeting to get feedback and make sure the output is aligned to business goals and is going to impact the outcome (mitigate churn rate). Depending on how this plan is shared, this step takes anywhere from a day to a week and is extremely crucial.

While the study takes place, partners are invited to observe sessions so they can see user pain points first hand. partners are also invited during the research debrief sessions to synthesize research findings and align on what are the top problems. UX Researchers then build a research presentation talking about the goals of the study, top findings and actionable recommendations that are presented to the partners.

Key Findings:

- Users felt overwhelmed by the amount of information presented during onboarding.
- The onboarding process lacked clear guidance on how to start learning.

- Users wanted to experience the core value of the app (language learning) more quickly.

Recommendations and Outcomes:

- **Simplify Onboarding:** Reduce the amount of information presented upfront and focus on the essential steps to get started.
- **Interactive Tutorial:** Introduce an interactive tutorial that guides users through the core features of the app in a hands-on way.
- **Early Success:** Allow users to experience a quick "win" early on (e.g., completing a short lesson) to demonstrate the app's value.

Integrating research into design

UX Researchers, after presenting the findings, can host solution workshops in collaboration with their design counterpart to

1. Make sure the designers understand the findings and have the information they need to start coming up with solutions. If there are gaps, UX

Researchers help translate those insights.
2. Ensure that the research findings don't stay on the shelf and are actually applied to inform design solutions

Testing solutions

Once solutions are built, UX Researchers might schedule another study to see if the new designs are solving user problems identified from the last round.

Case Study 2: Redesigning a Complex Enterprise Software Dashboard

Context:

A company that provides enterprise software for data analysis was receiving complaints that their dashboard was too complex and difficult to use. The UX researcher was brought in to help redesign the dashboard for improved usability.

Setting the scene

Similar to the last case study, UX Researcher

starts putting together a research plan. They also start scheduling meetings with the partners to understand business objectives, timeline by when research needs to be completed and any engineering timeline constraints they should be aware of.

Research Goals:

- Understand the mental models and workflows of users when interacting with the dashboard.
- Identify the key information users need to access and the tasks they need to perform.
- Develop recommendations for a redesigned dashboard that is more intuitive and efficient.

Research Process:

- **Contextual Inquiry:** Observed users in their natural work environment to understand how they use the dashboard in their daily tasks.
- **Card Sorting:** Used card sorting to understand users' mental models of how the information in the dashboard

should be organized.
- **Eye Tracking:** Employed eye tracking to identify users' visual attention patterns and areas of interest on the current dashboard.

Collaboration: Similar to the study above, this becomes a key milestone to bring partners in and share your research plan to get feedback and alignment. At this point you will want to make sure that your goals are answering business questions, the timeline by when research will be delivered is realistic and that everyone is aligned on the plan.

Key Findings:

- Users struggled to find the information they needed due to the overwhelming number of data points and complex visual hierarchy.
- The navigation and menu structure did not align with users' mental models.
- Users needed to perform repetitive actions to access commonly used features.

Recommendations and Outcomes:

- **Simplify Visual Design:** Reduce visual clutter, prioritize key information, and use clear visual cues to guide users' attention.
- **Improve Information Architecture:** Reorganize the dashboard based on users' mental models and workflows.
- **Streamline Interactions:** Reduce the number of clicks and steps required to complete common tasks.

These case studies illustrate how UX Researchers with academic backgrounds can apply their skills and knowledge to solve real-world problems in industry. By focusing on user needs, business goals, and data-driven decision-making, they can make a significant contribution to the success of their organizations.

CHAPTER 15:

TOOLS & RESOURCES

Starting your journey in UX research can feel overwhelming, but the right tools and resources can simplify the process and accelerate your growth. This chapter introduces essential UX research tools, recommended books and online learning platforms, and communities and conferences to help you connect with peers and industry experts.

There are more tools online than what I can list here. This is a short list of tools that have continuously been helpful to me and others I have known.

User Testing and Feedback

- UserTesting: Platform for remote usability testing with real users.
- Lookback: Allows you to record and

analyze user interactions in real-time.

- Optimal Workshop: Tools for card sorting, tree testing, and first-click testing.

Surveys and Questionnaires

- Google Forms: Free tool for creating and distributing surveys.
- Typeform: User-friendly platform for building engaging surveys.
- SurveyMonkey: Advanced survey tool with analytics and reporting features.

Prototyping and Wireframing

- Figma: Collaborative design tool for creating interactive prototypes.
- Adobe XD: Design and prototyping tool with intuitive features.
- Balsamiq: Low-fidelity wireframing tool for rapid design iterations.
- Google slides: A free to use tool to make prototypes. While not as sophisticated as other tools, it definitely does its job for low fidelity designs.

Analytics and Heatmaps

- Google Analytics: Tracks user behavior and engagement metrics.
- Hotjar: Provides heatmaps, session recordings, and feedback polls.
- Crazy Egg: Visualizes user behavior with heatmaps and scroll maps.

Data Analysis

- Excel/Google Sheets: Basic tools for organizing and analyzing data.
- NVivo: For qualitative data analysis and coding.
- Tableau: Data visualization software for creating interactive dashboards.
- Rainbow spreadsheet: Smashing magazine

Collaboration and Documentation

- Miro: Collaborative whiteboard for brainstorming and affinity mapping.
- Notion: All-in-one workspace for documenting and organizing research.
- Slack: Communication tool for team collaboration and sharing findings.

- Google docs: Research planning and collaboration with partners

Books, Blogs, and Online Courses

Books on UX Research

- “Don’t Make Me Think” by Steve Krug: A classic introduction to usability principles.
- “Observing the User Experience” by Elizabeth Goodman et al.: Comprehensive guide to UX research methods.
- “Think Like a UX Researcher” by David Travis and Philip Hodgson: Practical advice for conducting user research.
- “The User Experience Team of One” by Leah Buley: Tips for solo UX practitioners working with limited resources.
- “Interviewing Users” by Steve Portigal: In-depth guide to conducting effective user interviews.
- “The ethnographic interview” by James P. Spradley

Articles on UX research, usability, and

design principles.

Smashing Magazine:

- Website: https://www.smashingmagazine.com
- UX and web design insights, tutorials, and case studies.

UX Collective:

- Website: https://uxdesign.cc
- Community-driven platform with articles on UX research and design.

Baymard Institute:

- Website: Notion: All-in-one workspace for documenting and organizing research.

UX Matters:

- Website: https://uxmatters.com
- Covers a wide range of UX topics, including research methodologies.

Online Courses and Tutorials

Google:

- Course: Google UX Design certificate

- Platform: https://grow.google/certificates/ux-design/

Coursera:

- Course: “Introduction to User Experience Design” by Georgia Tech.
- Platform: https://www.coursera.org

Udemy:

- Course: “UX Research for Beginners.”
- Platform: https://www.udemy.com

Interaction Design Foundation (IDF):

- Course: “User Research – Methods and Best Practices.” Platform: https://www.interaction-design.org

LinkedIn Learning:

- Course: “Conducting UX Research Interviews.”
- Platform: https://www.linkedin.com/learning

Conclusion

Equipping yourself with the right tools, learning resources, and community support can significantly enhance your UX research capabilities. By exploring these options, you'll be better prepared to tackle challenges, improve user experiences, and grow in your career.

This concludes your journey through the essentials of UX research. Remember, every user insight brings you closer to creating impactful, user-centered designs. Keep learning, experimenting, and evolving as a UX researcher!

www.ingramcontent.com/pod-product-compliance
Lightning Source LLC
LaVergne TN
LVHW022204200926
848481LV00006B/1844
* 9 7 9 8 3 4 9 2 4 6 3 9 5 *